God's Living Oracles

God's Living Oracles

BEING THE

EXETER HALL LECTURES ON THE BIBLE

DELIVERED IN LONDON, ENGLAND
IN THE MONTHS OF JANUARY, FEBRUARY, MARCH
AND APRIL, 1903

By ARTHUR T. PIERSON

✠

NEW YORK: THE BAKER & TAYLOR CO.
33-37 East Seventeenth St., Union Sq., North

Printed at
The American Printing House
New York, U. S. A.

A Preliminary Word.

IN January, 1903, the writer of this book was asked to undertake what was proposed as a series of informal and conversational addresses in lower Exeter Hall, in London, before a body of a few hundred Christian workers and Bible students, accustomed to meet week by week for the study of Bible themes, and for further preparation for Christian work. The first address was delivered in the lower hall, but the available space was found so inadequate to the throng which attended, as to discourage the hope of increased audiences, and it was thought wise to give opportunity for a more extended hearing by holding subsequent meetings in a larger place; and, with some misgiving, the upper hall was opened for the purpose, but, after one or two additional lectures, well filled. There was plainly a hunger on the part of many for the Word of God, and God had obviously planned, unsuspected by man, that there should be both accommodation for a larger number of hearers, and an amplification of the originally proposed lines of address.

v

A Preliminary Word

These lectures were wholly informal, extemporaneous, and without written preparation; but it was suggested that they should be preserved and made procurable in a book form, and so reach many who did not hear them. The impulse of the author was to expand the original scheme of treatment, and undertake a more extended and exhaustive treatise on the theme; but this would have made the book too bulky, and almost wholly have destroyed the identity between the lectures as delivered and as printed. Moreover, the design of this discussion was not primarily to reach scholars, but rather, the ordinary hearers—the common folk. Brevity and simplicity are foremost qualities to be sought in such popular treatment, and hence, it has seemed best that the lectures as published should, as nearly as possible, reproduce the addresses as spoken. Whatever defects may be found in this volume, no one will be more aware of them than the author; but it is hoped that the contents of this book will be judged by their purpose and object, and not be subjected to unnecessarily minute criticism. Some facts and arguments presented here have been used in previous books from the same pen, but, if not new in form of statement, are at least in a new setting, and have a new bearing on other

A Preliminary Word

truths and arguments. The same facts and illustrations are susceptible of manifold uses.

The sole aim of this book is to awaken faith where it does not exist, and to strengthen and confirm it where it does; it is hoped, therefore, both to reach the honest doubter and to help believers, becoming the means of producing, or at least promoting, an intelligent and rational conviction that, in the Holy Scriptures we have God's Living Oracles, inspired by His Holy Spirit. It is devoutly hoped that, as in the Bible, Christ is the center and focus, He may be found in this book to hold the very shrine.

ARTHUR T. PIERSON.

Brooklyn, N. Y., 1127 Dean St., January, 1904.

Table of Contents

Table of Contents

God's Living Oracles

CHAPTER I

INTRODUCTORY

WHAT the heart of a fortress is to its outworks and minor defences, that, to the Christian Faith, is the Inspired Word of God—its central stronghold. To give up that, in any measure, is, therefore, in so far, to yield up the whole fortress to the foe.

Infidelity and irreligion seem now to be massing all their united forces for a combined and final assault upon the whole system of Christianity, and there are signs of a subtle, ingenious and Satanic plot to undermine its very foundations by destroying all belief in the supernatural. All intelligent faith in the supernatural rests, ultimately, upon the divine origin, plenary inspiration and infallible authority of the Bible, as the Book of God; and hence, naturally and necessarily, this book becomes the very center both of the attack and the defence.

Such facts at such a crisis constitute a challenge to the believer to examine anew into the whole question whether there be ample evidence of the super-human authorship of this book, carefully to weigh its claims to divine authority, and to determine how far it utters a judgment and verdict from which there is no appeal. In such matters, doubt is disaster, for even an honest misgiving is destructive both of intellectual conviction and moral repose, unsettling, if not undermining, the very basis upon which rests human confidence in the stability of a structure, the like of which never was reared. On the other hand, whatever confirms and establishes faith in the Living Oracles of God correspondingly affects every interest dearest to the believer and to mankind. If intelligent investigation produces certainty of conviction, the results are manifold: the whole history of Christianity for nearly two thousand years is vindicated; fresh force is imparted to all holy living and new nerve is infused into modern missions at home and abroad, while such faith in the Bible inspires a grand hope for all coming ages. The remote results are correspondingly grand; for, in proportion as, in this generation, confidence in the Word of God is confirmed, generations, yet unborn, will feel more assured that they have a rock basis for their creed and conduct.

The subject calls for calm, candid, patient investigation. Rhetorical emphasis cannot be made to do duty for rational conviction, invective cannot supply the lack of intelligence, nor can abuse of those who are believed to be in error, take the place of the sound argument that compels conviction and grounds believers in the truth. In a game, he who only stands on the defensive, loses; in battle, victory seldom comes to an army that only hides behind entrenchments; and what is needed for the vindication of Christianity is that we shall not simply be able to hold our own, but to carry the war into the enemy's territory. Men demand not negations but positions—positive proofs that the Bible is of God, proofs that will bear the searchlight and stand severe tests. It will not do for faith to be indistinguishable from credulity. God never meant that the believer's confidence in His word should be a blind bigoted assumption of what is unproven, hiding behind ignorance, tradition or superstition. If the Bible be a divine book, it has nothing to fear from rational inquiry. Investigation will issue in vindication, and the more searching the investigation, the more triumphant the vindication.

A few years ago a party of five, roped together, were climbing a precipitous cliff in the Alps. At a critical point in the ascent, the lowermost man lost foothold, and dragged after him the next above, and so on, till the increased strain caused all the party to lose their foothold except the leader, who, driving his axe and alpenstock into the ice, and bracing himself firmly, enabled the man, next below, to regain his footing, and so successively each of the four once more recovered himself, because the foremost man had stood the strain. It is not too much to say that, while the Word of God holds its place firmly in the minds and hearts of men, as God's own book, inbreathed of the Holy Spirit and to be believed and trusted in every part as a divine guide to doctrine and duty, all that is most precious in our Christian faith and life holds its place in our convictions and confidence; but that, if the Bible loses or loosens its hold upon us as an infallible standard of truth and duty, everything else goes down with it into the same abyss of doubt. For, let it be remembered, the Word of God is the Revelation of Jesus Christ, of the Holy Ghost, of the nature and secrets of all spiritual life; without it we have no authentic history of Jesus the Saviour, no knowledge of the way of salvation, no unfolding of the mystery of Godliness, no clear unveiling of a future life.

It is common, in these days, carelessly to say that, even if the Bible were taken from the believer, he cannot be separated from Christ who, by the Spirit of God, dwells within him; and hence it is argued that, while it is of supreme consequence to possess Christ, it is not needful to be concerned as to whether or not the Word of God be infallibly inspired. This fallacy is too shallow to deceive or mislead a thoughtful disciple; for it by no means follows that, after one has safely reached a secure resting-place, it is of no consequence what becomes of the road thither by which he traveled. Is one to feel no concern for those who are to come after and who will be dependent on finding a plain path to the same goal? Only a madman or a monster would be indifferent to the obliteration of all the marks, blazed on the trees of a dense forest or dangerous jungle, for the guidance of lost travelers, because he himself had got into the open fields beyond. Were every Bible burned, and the teaching of that Book blotted out from the literature of mankind, how is another soul of man to know with any certainty, of Christ, of salvation by grace, of the Holy Spirit, and of the new birth in Him, of the plan of God for worldwide missions, of Christian stewardship, of the second advent of our Lord, and of the future state with its final awards?

For such reasons, among many others, it is first of all needful for all believers to have an intelligent, rational, unshakable confidence in God's Word as divine in origin, inspired of the Holy Spirit, a safe guide in belief and a sure pattern for practice. We say an intelligent and reasonable faith. "What do you believe?" asked Whitefield of a Roman Catholic worker in the coal pits of Cornwall. "What the Church believes," was the answer. "And what does the Church believe?" "What I believe." "And what do you both believe?" *"The same thing."*

Fides carbonaria—the "collier's faith"—has long been ridiculed as a specimen of blind credulity. To believe only what, and only because, others believe, may be perpetuating false teaching, helping on what Cyprian called *vetustam erroris*— the old age of error.

The Spirit of God enjoins disciples to "be ready always to give an answer to every one that asketh a reason for the hope" that is within them. (1 Peter: III:15.) The more intelligent and reasonable faith is, therefore, the more pleasing and honouring to God, the more helpful to men, and the more restful and forceful to oneself.

The interests of truth demand that we should take even a stronger and more advanced position. The presumption is against the Bible's claims, rather than in their favour. Every prominent false religion affirms the possession of sacred books, and virtually claims a divine origin; the Word of God, therefore, must vindicate its right to be accepted, while others are rejected, and prove its worthiness to hold the supreme place in man's confidence as the one unique, incomparable Book of God. It is true that for thousands of years this Book has, by common consent of disciples, been held to be divine; yet even this fact cannot, of itself, establish its right to intelligent acceptance. Every man and woman should so examine for themselves as to know why they receive this one book as entitled to the preëminence in both intellect and heart, swaying thoughts, affections and will.

God has constituted and capacitated human beings to weigh evidence, because He means that they shall use their faculties in ascertaining what is true and false, and what is right and wrong. Man is to weigh, in the scales of the reason, whatever claims allegiance as truth, and subject it to the test of searching scrutiny, that he may separate between truth and falsehood. Then he is to weigh, in the scales of conscience, whatever claims obedience as duty, and try it by the standard of moral excellence, that he may discriminate between right and wrong. What reason approves as true, and conscience sanctions as right, the will is prepared to embrace; for the judgment gives its decision, that such matters are to be held as convictions and followed as practices. Not only does the Bible never avoid or evade such tests, but it challenges men to apply them; courting the severest search, and claiming obedience only when investigation has first established its right to confidence as the authoritative Word of God.

The phrase, "Oracles of God," occurs four times in the New Testament, and the instances are significant.* Here four things are to be noted: first, they are called "living"; second, they are received from God, and committed in custody to men to be given to others, the fact of such entrustment constituting the supreme "advantage" or privilege of the Jew; third, these oracles contain and inculcate certain "first principles"; and fourth, it is to be the supreme aim of every preacher and teacher to be guided by them in his utterance. These four passages thus furnish an illustration of the way in which the Word of God supplies the reader with a guide to its own interpretation. Here is a body of divine communications or revelations. They are endowed with living and life-giving power, they announce great first principles for our belief and

*Acts vii: 38.   The Living Oracles.   Romans iii: 2; Heb. v:12; 1 Peter iv: 11.

8

Introductory

practise, and they should control all our speech and conduct in behalf of God.

The lines to be pursued in the following pages are thus laid down at the beginning. Taking for granted that, if the Bible be the Book of God, it contains within itself ample proofs of its divine origin, and satisfactory evidence to support its claims, let it be the joint endeavour of the writer and the reader to approach the subject with a candid mind and a pure conscience. Both intellectual and moral honesty are first requisites in such a study. The vision of man is binocular. He needs the clear seeing eye of the understanding and the equally unobscured insight of the heart, to read aright the Book of God. The intellectual and moral faculties should be focused upon the Divine Word, if its character and claims are to be intelligently and candidly examined and weighed. With such conditions attending the investigation, two marked results are sure to follow: first, the Bible will not be invested with a false halo, which, as the incense of superstitious worshippers obscures their idol, hinders clearness of vision; and, secondly, whatever be its real character and essential glory, it will be seen and acknowledged. The same law that forbids a blind credulity, prohibits an equally blind prejudice. An honest examination makes it alike impossible to believe without proofs and to withhold faith when the evidence is adequate. While truth has nothing to fear from the most searching tests, no tests can satisfy him in whom truth is not enthroned. God therefore "desires truth in the inward parts." Light appears and appeals only to the seeing and open eye.

CHAPTER II

THE BIBLE AS A BOOK

THE literary element in the Oracles of God naturally first claims attention. We have to do with a book.

In nature there are conspicuous phenomena which demand explanation. The boulder is such a phenomenon. Whether or not man's science can satisfactorily account for it, the boulder is an indisputable fact and as such must be dealt with.* The science would be blind, and the philosophy folly, that would deny or dispute its existence.

In the world of letters, there are also phenomena which call for investigation and explanation, and foremost among them all is this grand Book. Hitherto human science and philosophy have failed to account for it on any purely natural basis. Nevertheless the Bible is a fact, no less to be denied than the boulder. Within its pages may be found its own explanation. It claims to be a supernatural revelation. If this theory be accepted it adequately accounts for the book, and the

*Prof. Barbour of Glasgow.

important question is, is the Bible's explanation of itself to be accepted as true?

It is necessary to look carefully at this literary phenomenon, viewing it from every side, in order to appreciate both its real greatness and the need of some extraordinary method of accounting for its existence, character, survival through the ages, and influence among men.

By universal concession and confession, this is the one Book of the ages, altogether unique and wholly unrivalled. Hence, its name "The Bible," attributed to "John of the golden mouth." At a time when all literature was but in its beginning, appeared a book that rather befits the ending. When the foundation for the pyramid of letters was being laid, there was brought forth one stone of matchless symmetry, itself a little pyramid, the only fit apex to complete and crown the whole structure, a capstone whose lines and angles might well determine the dimensions and proportions, lines and angles of the pyramid. Whence came this capstone, while as yet the cornerstone of literature was scarce laid? In what quarry was it found and by what hand was it hewn? It is, moreover, of no common material, but a precious stone, a colossal gem, the like of which is found in none of the richest quarries or mines of the earth.

The Bible as a Book

Thus to describe the Bible is not merely to indulge in the poetry of rhetoric, but to state the most prosaic fact. This is the one book, which neither belongs to nor befits the infancy of the race, and yet it was found among men in the early days of the world's history; and, with all the boasted learning and wisdom of the twentieth century, it still defies all competition. The philosopher and sage cannot equal it, neither shall it be exchanged for all the jewels and fine gold of the noblest poetry and richest products of the imagination.

Human hands had indeed to do with it. Scores of different writers contributed to its pages; but this, instead of accounting for it, rather deepens our perplexity as to its origin, unless there was manifestly, behind and above these human composers and compilers, some one true author who at least superintended and controlled the whole. Great Cathedrals, like those of Milan and Cologne, occupied centuries in building. Hundreds and thousands of workmen wrought upon them. Generations gave their successive relays of labourers who hoisted the marble blocks to their places and built up walls and buttresses, pillars and arches, spires and pinnacles. Surely no one needs to be told that, behind and beyond these builders, there must have been some one architect who built the fane in his own mind before the cornerstone was laid; who, first of all, drew the plans and furnished even the minute specifications; so that such a structure owes its matchless symmetry, not to the men of brawn that worked on it, but to that one man of brain that thought out the cathedral in its completeness, and whose detailed plans directed the day-labourers in their work.

The Bible is a stately cathedral. Many human builders have in turn wrought on the structure. Who is the architect? What one mind is that which planned and saw the whole building, before Moses wrote those first words of Genesis, which by no accident, as though to carve the architect's name on the vestibule, are these: "IN THE BEGINNING GOD."

Does the Bible, considered as a book, demand a divine author? To answer this, it behooves us, first, to look carefully at some of its leading characteristics, as a book, to examine it as a literary product and an achievement in the world of letters.

This question—whether the literary character of the Book comports with its claim to a divine authorship, is the natural vestibule by which the student approaches the inner teachings and contents of the Oracles of God.

One should make sure, as he treads this threshold

that he brings to his investigation that first of all requisites, already referred to—a candid mind. Candor is a rare quality. We repeat by way of emphasis that many a truth is seen falsely, or not at all, because of defects in the mental or moral vision. Few have an unbiased mind, so open to conviction as to be prepared to weigh proofs with absolute impartiality, and to admit the full force of evidence, even when it upsets former convictions and disproves former conclusions. Bigotry hates light. Prejudice only contracts the mental eye as light is poured upon it, and may even close it so as to shut out the rays entirely. In order to form safe and sound opinions, it is necessary to lay aside prejudices and prepossessions, alike, so as to look at plain facts, and give them their full value. It is well also to bear in mind Paley's maxim, never to let what we do not know disturb our confidence as to what we do know; and Butler's still wiser proverb, that, if a fact is once settled, objections cannot unsettle it; for the fact rests on our knowledge, but the objections on our ignorance.

Here then is a remarkable literary phenomenon to be accounted for; if in any natural human way, by all means that should suffice: the "Law of Parsimony," or "Economy of Force," forbids needless admission of a miracle. But, if this greatest of books cannot be accounted for satisfactorily upon a purely natural and human basis, we are driven to accept its own self-explanation and concede the mysterious supernatural and superhuman element which it claims.

The Bible is assumed to be a phenomenon, wholly unrivalled in the world of letters, since, even its enemies being judges, this is not denied.

One of its most important features is its *unity*, and as marvellous as it is conspicuous. Every circumstance connected with its preparation and production, was calculated to prevent and prohibit such unity. Here are sixty-six different books, written by some forty different authors, in three different languages, and the periods of authorship cover a score or more of centuries. These human writers were brought up in different countries, and were so remote from each other in time and space, that they could have had no mutual acquaintance, and could neither have conspired for an evil end nor combined for the best purpose. The subjects on which they wrote were very diverse and various, some historical, some prophetical, some devotional, some ethical. The form of their writings was in some cases prose and in others poetry, and yet, notwithstanding all these divergent elements, they have produced essentially one book. Not only is the

Bible as a whole an unrivalled phenomenon, but its features are all phenomenal, and none more so than this convergence of contents like rays toward one common focal point.

As the reader takes up this Book, he finds, first of all, that it is in two parts, known as the Old and New Testaments. But each of these is multiplex and complex: in the Old Testament are thirty-nine parts, and in the New, twenty-seven. Yet, when these two Testaments are examined more closely, in each is found a historic, ethic and prophetic element. The historic gives the annals, or outline of events; the ethic adds the moral and spiritual teaching necessary for guidance in practical life, and the prophetic forecasts the future. Taking the three together, the reader finds, spread before him, past history, present duty, and future destiny.

This unity reaches not only to all great matters, but even to most minute details. The grand moral and spiritual lessons, by whomsoever taught, or in whatsoever way, essentially agree. Certain conspicuous conceptions or ideas pervade the whole book, like golden cords on which all else is strung—such as the ideas of the Kingdom of God, sin and salvation, sacrifice and priesthood. Many of these conceptions are so lofty and unique in sublimity and novelty, that it is impossible to account for them on any human theory. They are not the product of the times in which these men wrote, nor are the like found in any other literature of those or subsequent periods; moreover, for some of them no adequate words could be found then in use among men, so that old words and phrases had to be invested with a new meaning; as for instance, holiness, humility, love. In not a few cases, the conceptions were even paradoxical: they seemed to involve contradiction if not absurdity; yet they were too grand and awe-inspiring to be set aside as mere vagaries of ignorance and foolishness, as for instance, the idea of eternity—endless duration without succession—or of absolute sovereignty which decrees all events, yet both allows and ordains freedom of choice and action; or the idea of a trinity in the Godhead without plurality of Gods, and many other like conceptions which seem above the mind of man to originate, or even to comprehend when suggested.

The unity of the Bible is absolutely unique. Never elsewhere have so many different treatises, historical, biographical, ethical, prophetical, poetical, been combined together, making one book, as all the hewn stone and timber make one building, or better still, as all the bones, muscles and ligaments combine in one body. This again, while indisputable as a fact, is unparalled in literature, all the conditions being, humanly speaking, not only unfavourable, but fatal to such combination.

Wherever else we find diversity of writers, we expect diversity of matter, each writer having his own character, or individuality, reaching into all departments of his being and work. As no two faces or forms are precisely alike, the individual features of mind and heart are yet more marked. Charles the Fifth found that he could not even make two watches run exactly together, much less make two men think or feel alike. Temperaments differ. Dispositions, like lenses, magnify or minify or color whatever is seen through them. These natural peculiarities, inborn, are also inbred. Education, instead of removing, develops and intensifies them, making absolute uniformity and agreement the more impossible. The whole tendency of growth is from unity toward diversity. Society is a plant that, the more it grows, the more it branches and minutely ramifies. Men are kept alike only by keeping them from growing, and even then, the similarity is only seeming. The freedom that knocks off fetters and leaves them free to think and speak, also leaves them free to develop independence and individuality. The writers of the Bible have all the marks of individuality. How different Moses from Malachi, Isaiah from Daniel, James from John, Peter from Paul! This diversity of nature cannot but betray itself in style, which, as Buffon said, "*is* the man;" language, Wordsworth called the "incarnation of thought," expression of feeling and words taking on all the varieties of the inner life.

Diversity of times, places and circumstances would ordinarily make unity impossible. These many writers belong to different generations, centuries and ages in human history. They lived in different lands. Their surroundings were various, they spoke different languages, were moulded in the matrix of diverse national life. How different a life of exile in Babylon from one of pilgrimage in the desert, or a home in Judea; how opposite the associations of the herdsman of Tekoa and the cupbearer in the Persian court! How far off in periods were Ezra in Jerusalem and John in Patmos; Moses in Egypt and Paul in Rome!

The diversity in subject matter is more striking. In this one book may be found every variety of theme that can well be imagined, from the story of creation to the forecast of the new creation. Here is endless diversity—fragments of national history, and of individual biography, poems and

speeches, proverbs and predictions, parables and
ethical teachings, legal enactments and elaborate
ritual, romances of love and awful tragedies of
judgment, plain precepts for right living, and
spectacular dramatic scenes, gorgeously painted
in oriental imagery; miracles and mysteries, the
prattle of a child, side by side with the profoundest
discourses of philosophers and sages.

All this diversity of subject implies corresponding variety in the immediate object or purpose in
view.   These various books were written to serve
different ends.   Sometimes they set forth the will
of God as to daily life, and sometimes unfold His
great plans for the race.   Here are lyrics, intended
to express and guide a devotional spirit; and again,
stories of suffering to illustrate the victory of faith
and rewards of patience.   The evangelists give a
fourfold portrait of Christ; and the Epistles apply
His teachings to the current needs and perils of
existing churches.   The book of Joshua is a book
of the wars of the Lord; Solomon's Song is a
dramatic love poem, and its scene, a court.   The
book of Judges treats of a period of semi-anarchy;
the Acts, of a generation of primitive church life.
No two of these treatises cover the same ground.
The diversity, which, in any other book, would be
fatal to unity—here, somehow, contributes to it,

as a great variety of stones, of all forms, shapes and colours, combine in an exquisite mosaic. Does not such a mosaic argue a master hand that artistically arranges the stones according to a preconceived pattern?

In many other ways or forms this unity appears, and all are remarkable. Further examples may be found in some facts, generally overlooked, of which two may be mentioned.

1. The first mention of a number, person, place or subject usually, if not uniformly, determines its general usage afterward, and its relation to the entire remainder of the book. When we first meet the number "seven," it stands for a completed work, and a period of rest. Throughout the Bible that number seems to represent essentially the same conceptions. The first mention of the Spirit of God is in connection with brooding, like a dove, over the watery abyss to bring life and order out of chaos. From that point on, this seems to be His special work—a sort of maternal office, brooding over the chaos of a ruined race to develop celestial order, life and beauty. The first time the words, "believe", "counted" and "righteousness" appear, either separately or together, is in connection with the statement that Abram "believed in the Lord and it was counted unto him

for righteousness."* From that point on, faith and the imputation of righteousness are indissolubly linked. This law of "first mention" is so conspicuous that it supplies a sort of lexicon of biblical terms, giving the reader of Genesis a key to the meaning of the whole Scripture and making the Bible its own commentary. Yet it is plain that, without supernatural guidance, the writer who first used words or phrases in such a collection could not have forecast the subsequent use and application by other writers of the terms he used.

2. Again, it is essential in a book which is practically the guide for the faith and life of millions of men, that every great subject having to do with daily duty should have adequate treatment. Somewhere, between Genesis and Revelation, every such matter is treated, comprehensively and exhaustively, and usually once for all, very few instances of repetition occurring.

For instance, there is but one comprehensive portrait of charity (1 Cor. XIII). The power of the tongue is once exhaustively treated (James, III). Once for all the dual nature of the God-man is fully set before us (Hebrews: I, II). The laws and principles of Christian giving are found in 2 Cor. VIII, IX. God's search for lost souls is set forth

*Gen. xv: 6.

especially in Luke xv by a three-fold parable, and the mysteries of the kingdom in Matthew xiii in a series of seven parables. The last judgment of the great white throne is found only in Rev. xx. Faith, its nature and victories, only with any fulness in Hebrews xi, xii. There is no complete discourse on the resurrection except in 1 Cor. xv. The last discourse and intercessory prayer of our Lord, only in John xiv-xvii. Romans vi-viii is one complete discussion of the question, "Shall we continue in sin?" There is no such chapter elsewhere as the twenty-first of Numbers, the twelfth of Exodus, or the thirty-eighth of Job, or the fifty-third of Isaiah. The present rest of faith is treated only in Heb. iii: 7 to iv: 11. And the final community of the redeemed finds adequate treatment only in Rev. xxi-xxii.

All this implies divine foresight. Humanly speaking, no writer could have foreseen what topics would be covered in the writings of other contributors to the body of Scripture. Yet we find, scattered throughout this sacred Book, monographs, each singularly complete in itself, and each making any other on the same subject unnecessary. While apparently there is no arrangement, yet there is obviously a consummate plan, by which all needs are met, yet none oversupplied.

The Bible as a Book

It would be impossible to find any great matter on which information and instruction are needed which is not somewhere treated satisfactorily; and, whatever fragmentary teachings may be found scattered through the Word, there is some one place where these isolated precepts are gathered together and combined, and the full truth on any great subject is taught.

The unity of the Bible constitutes, in and of itself, a conclusive proof of its supernatural and superhuman origin. It is difficult even to suppose a case of a similar character. Any such a volume, if compiled at all, would not be homogeneous but heterogeneous, the only unity being that mechanical unity dependent on the binder who puts together in one cover literary productions having no common point of view, plan of treatment, or unity of theme. In this one Book the impossible is actual and real, and the unity is the more remarkable because it is manifold.

This unity is structural; the Bible is built up on a definite plan. In the New Testament the four Gospel narratives are not mere repetitions, but designed to present as many aspects of the life and career of the Lord Jesus Christ; then the book of the Acts immediately follows, showing what He continued to do and to teach by the Holy Spirit in the Church, and how the Pentecostal Baptism prepared the Church for her witnessing career in Judea, Samaria, and then among Romans and Greeks.

The Gospel narratives appear to stand substantially in the order of composition; but manifestly here is a divine design. The gospel according to Matthew, written for the Hebrew mind, must come first, for it links on the Old Testament to the New, and for two reasons: first, because the Hebrew race forms the grand center of Old Testament history; and, second, because the Messiah was of the Jews and the consummate flower of the Jewish genealogical tree. Mark, the companion of Peter, obviously addresses the Latin mind, the Gentiles, particularly Romans, as was fitting, for, in the book of the Acts, Peter was appointed first to open the door of faith to the Romans. Then follows Luke, who, as Paul's companion, would naturally write also for Gentiles, but especially for *Greeks*, among whom Paul's ministry was so largely spent. John's narrative supplements all the others, and has the most catholic aim and character, and appeals to the human race as such and to believers generally without regard to nationality.

There are five Epistle writers, Paul especially the Apostle of Faith, Peter, of Hope, John, of Love,

James, of Good Works, and Jude, of Warning against Apostasy. Thus, without human design, or intentional coöperation, all the necessary ground is covered without overlapping.

The unity is diadactic and ethical. There is no inconsistency in the moral teaching from beginning to end; or, if at first any is apparent, a further and more careful examination reveals harmony, as the two pictures in the stereoscope blend together when once the proper focus is found by the eye. The whole Bible consistently teaches, on the basis of natural religion, with creation as its cornerstone, an original and universal fatherhood of God and brotherhood of Man; but that only on the basis of spiritual redemption, with the new creation as its cornerstone, is found again the true fatherhood or brotherhood which sin lost or forfeited. Around these dual conceptions of man's natural and spirtual relations to God and his fellowman, all ethical teaching of the Bible moves. Part of man's relation and duty to his fellowman originates in the fact that all are "offspring" of God, by nature; but the higher level, both of obligation and privilege, is reached only when, born from above, men become partakers of the divine nature, and children of God by faith in Christ Jesus. Then is recognized a new relation to the household of faith and a new motive and reason is felt for doing good unto all men.

This unity is historic. The Bible, however, is not a history of the race, but rather of the kingdom of God. It centers about a chosen family, the family of Abraham, and so a chosen nation—Israel. It follows this people till they become apostate. After this, the historic thread is dropped, and not resumed until it is caught up prophetically in the predicted restoration of Israel. The long interval covering the "Times of the Gentiles" has no proper record in this book, and other nations incidentally appear in the narrative only or mainly as related to this chosen nation, Israel, and the kingdom of God under Messiah.

This unity is prophetic. Here again Israel and the kingdom of God form the central idea. Adam, the original creation king, lost his sceptre in the fall and Satan obtained it by right of conquest. The Second Man, espousing Adam's cause, overcame his victor, and so regained the lost sceptre; and in Him—the last Adam—the restored kingdom will stand forever and the gates of hell shall not prevail against it. All prophecy ultimately relates to this new King, the Divine Head of the Adamic race, and to His kingdom; to His first coming and its militant period, to His second coming and its triumphant period. Other parties are referred to as the foes of God and His people, such as Nineveh, Egypt, Babylon, Tyre, etc., in former days—the beast, false prophet, Babylon and the dragon, in the latter days.

The unity is mathematic. A numerical system obviously pervades the Bible; and, although its full meaning or final object is not yet disclosed to us or discerned by us, certain conclusions seem safe. For example, the mathematical forms which pervade the Word of God, appear to be the triangle, square and circle, with the corresponding pyramid, cube and sphere. According to the conclusions of those who have most carefully studied the numerical system of Scripture, the numbers which seem to have special significance are, *one*, as the symbol of unity; *two*, of contrast or confirmation; *three*, of the Trinity; *four*, of the world and space; *seven*, which as the sum of three and four, is the natural expression of completeness and rest; *ten*, the sum of the first four numbers, expressive of completeness by successive additions—and hence one of the numbers of *time; twelve*, the multiple of three and four, expressing the penetration or pervasion of the human by the divine, etc. This may hint the reason why *forty* so often appears—the multiple of four and ten—the numbers of time and space; and seventy, a

complete time period; and 144,000—the cube of ten
multiplied into the square of twelve. Reverent
and humble students of the Bible hesitate to claim
peculiar insight into the mystery of Bible numbers;
but the uniformity of their use, by various writers,
compels the belief that the great Mathematician
of the Universe was behind such use. Here alone
there opens an almost untrodden field for boundless investigation and possible discovery.

This unity, which we have found to be structural,
seems also to be *organic*, the unity of a living
organism, in which there is a pervasive, vitalizing
spirit, making all parts living members and organs,
all necessary to the whole body and to each other.
Of the biblical body of truth, as of the mystical
Body of Christ, it is therefore true that no part can
say to another, "I have no need of thee," and that
those members which seem to be feeble, or less
honorable, are equally necessary to the complete
body, and have a God-given honor in supplying
what otherwise would be a lack.

In the human body, careful investigation shows
that right and left eyes, ears, hands and feet hold a
mutually complementary relation, and are meant
to work together; so the various books of the Bible
sustain a mutual relation. Let anyone compare
the opening verses of Genesis, of the Gospel accord-

ing to John, and of the first Epistle of John; let him read, side by side, Leviticus and Hebrews; Joshua and the Acts of the Apostles; the Epistles of Paul and of James; Ezekiel, Daniel and the Apocalypse; Judges and Jude; Ruth and Solomon's Song, Exodus and the two letters to the Corinthians. Let the careful student diligently compare the four Gospel narratives, and examine their points of likeness and unlikeness; and the more diligent his study is, the more will he see that one consummately comprehensive plan pervades this organism in which every member has its ministry, and that not one book could be spared without maiming the Body of the Word.

In an organic body, all parts are necessary to its completeness, though not equally important in their prominence and service. When one part, however small, is gone, there is what is called mayhem, a defective body, and no artificial substitute can make the body complete. Certain parts of the body are called vital parts by way of distinction; other parts may be lost and the body live; but if these are gone, death ensues.

Most important of all, the unity is personal and Messianic. One grand Personage is the Living Sun about which all planets and their satellites revolve. For Him, the Living Word, the Written

31

Word was framed. Like the strange star which Eastern magi saw, the Bible has a special mission as to Christ: it burns with His borrowed Light, it guides all seekers to Him, it rests over Him, it loses in His glory its own lustre, and in Him finds alike its explanation and its end.

Some of the statements hitherto made in brief are subsequently to be expanded and illustrated. It seemed well, however, to group together in this manner the various leading features of the Bible as a book among books; but, thus early in the investigation, candor constrains the confession that, however the Bible may be accounted for, it stands not only without superior, but without equal or rival, as a literary product beyond comparison, towering in solitary grandeur above all other writings of men.

This is the first stage reached in our study. Both in the order of time and merit, this book stands confessedly first, not only prominent, but preëminent. The book of Job is the earliest and the finest of dramatic poems. No devout lyrics can match the Psalms of David, no proverbs equal those of Solomon, no prophetic visions those of Isaiah and Ezekiel, no ethical precepts those of Christ. What biography was ever so short and sublime as that of Enoch: "He walked with God and he was not, for God took him?" Where is such a portrait of love as in 1 Corinthians XIII, or such exhibition of gratitude for forgiveness as in Luke VII, or such humility as in John XIII? Can all literature furnish two parables equal to those in Luke xv and John xv?

What wonder is it if the believer feels that, even considered as a literary product, this Book is superhuman?

CHAPTER III

THE BIBLE AND SCIENCE

THE Oracles of God must have some relation, however indirect, to truth at large. The God of all truth cannot, in any of His utterances, contradict Himself. His kingdom cannot stand and be divided against itself. Manifestly His works and His word must, in all essentials, agree. Hence the question as to the attitude of the Bible toward science cannot be avoided.

There is a scientific element in the Word of God, though it is not in any proper sense a scientific treatise, and for obvious reasons should not be; since there is no need of any supernatural revelation of scientific facts, which may be ascertained in natural ways. God would neither waste miraculous energy on His own part, nor encourage on man's part, intellectual indolence and inertia. Moreover, the reception of scientific truth by man is partly dependent on its discovery by man; the research which ultimately unvails the mysteries of nature, meanwhile develops in the investigators the capacity for the apprehension and appreciation of such truth when disclosed. Ignorance is naturally blind, only intelligence being open-eyed; and it is this painstaking study of the facts and phenomena of nature which transforms ignorance into intelligence, and so endows man with scientific vision.

If God, in the Bible, plainly pre-announced scientific facts, He would therefore, be unwise and self-contradictory; and such pre-announcement would be harmful rather than useful, perplexing the reader, raising controversy, dividing human opinion and discrediting divine revelation.

While all this may be fairly conceded, on the other hand, the God of the Bible, being also the God of nature, it is equally plain that, on whatever theme the Omniscient One speaks, even incidentally and casually, He must be at home. When a thoroughly educated man writes a history, his culture appears even in incidental references to other departments of knowledge, such as geography and astronomy, and his education will be seen even in his grammar and spelling. The All-knowing God cannot be supposed to betray ignorance on any subject, nor the God of all truth to lend Himself to falsehood. The Bible claims ivine authorship. Infinite veracity cannot lend nction to what is essentially erroneous, nor can omniscience conceal itself behind the veil of popular illusion and delusion, prevailing superstition, or careless inaccuracy.

Certain propositions seem both to be self-evident, and to deserve to be put boldly at the front in all discussion of the attitude of the Bible toward science:

1. The Bible is not, and could not, in the nature of things, be, primarily, a scientific book.

2. Were it such it would impugn the wisdom of its divine author, and discredit its divine origin.

3. Incidentally, and unavoidably, however, it must touch upon the realm of science.

4. God, the only Infallible Scientist, cannot be supposed to make mis-statements, or exhibit ignorance.

While these are self-evident propositions, it follows that, as some reference to scientific facts is inevitable, there must be a skillful management of such references, so that, without losing sight of its primary purpose as a moral and spiritual guide, the Bible shall not, at any point, be in conflict with essential truth.

The following additional statements, which we are prepared to defend, also indicate the general line of the discussion which follows:

1. Without anticipating, directly, scientific dis-

covery, Biblical language, properly interpreted, does not contradict established facts.

2. A poetic phraseology is often used, which by the flexibility of figurative or imaginative terms, allows room for expansion and accommodation to facts when known.

3. Tested by cosmogony, astronomy, geology and zoölogy, physiology and comparative anatomy, natural philosophy and sanitary science, etc., this Book evinces superhuman knowledge and wisdom.

4. Hence the Bible is a scientific marvel. It belongs to the oldest class of literature, yet it is the youngest and newest in adaptation to scientific discovery, and perpetually keeps abreast of human progress.

Close examination reveals what might be expected, if this is God's book—divine ingenuity in solving the problem already indicated. Infinite wisdom devised a middle path between pre-announcement of scientific facts and laws, and endorsement of current errors and absurdities. The elastic phraseology employed is susceptible of a new and broader interpretation as new facts come to light, which demand such accommodation. In some instances popular language is used which is not technically accurate, and yet such language does not indicate "error," being perfectly admissible, because *true to facts of appearance*. With the foremost modern scientists it is both customary and accounted proper to describe such natural phenomena without so correcting the terms used as to conform strictly and technically to scientific standards. The most learned natural philosopher does not hesitate to speak of the sun's rising and the horizon's sinking, though both are due to the earth's axial revolution, and are only facts of appearance. Similar latitude may properly be claimed for the Word of God, which conforms its language to such facts of appearance, where no essential error is involved.

The final conclusion to which we are compelled to come is that the scientific terms used in the Bible constitute a part of the Oracles of God, such language being itself oracular or essentially parabolic, hiding the truth in enigma—mysteriously enfolding a germ of scientific fact, which subsequent research is to unfold, expand, and invest with a new, true and unsuspected scientific meaning. These statements a few examples will suffice to illustrate, and so to vindicate:

1. The mother of all the sciences is COSMOGONY, the science of creation. Man's first question, as he opens his eyes intelligently upon the universe of matter, is, "How came all this to be? and when?

38

and by whom? Out of this as natural offspring come all the other questions as to the physical constitution of the universe and the mystery of planetary and stellar worlds: the constitution of man and his complex nature and being; of the lower animals, and their various ranks in the scale of being; of plants, and the mystery of vegetable life; and the constitution of the earth with its material forms and forces. The study of cosmogony leads also to the more general and comprehensive science of natural philosophy, which deals with the phenomena of life, light, heat, motion, and all forms or manifestations of force in the universe, with the grand laws which govern them.

As to Cosmogony, this mother of all sciences, one brief sublime sentence in the opening verse of the Bible, grandly declares:

"IN THE BEGINNING GOD CREATED THE HEAVENS AND THE EARTH."

There was, then, a beginning: when, it is not said; but back of that beginning was One who had no beginning. Creation had a Creator. This one short sentence of ten words is yet so pregnant with divine meaning that, after thousands of years, men are yet finding in it new and grander significances.

How many errors are here corrected! "In the

beginning"—the fact that there was a beginning contradicts the eternity of matter. "In the beginning, God"—that refutes atheism. It was *one* God, not many,—that knocks over polytheism. "God created"—that forbids the doctrine of chance. God is separate from creation—that precludes pantheism. Matter is not God,—that denies materialism. As we enter the vestibule of this book the first five words of the ten meet us with a complete denial of the false philosophies of the ages.

How far this story of the genesis of all things is abreast of modern science, every new approach to absolute and final truth is continually revealing. Infidels have sought to make irreconcilable contradiction where a reverent reader will discover the most singular and surprising correspondence.

A quotation from a very recent volume may furnish an example:

"So far as the material universe is concerned, the two primary factors were *matter* and *motion* as manifestations of persistent force. Besides these two modes we think of phenomena also in relation to their sequences, and in relation to their co-existences. The former of these two modes we call "time" and the latter "space." Mr. Herbert Spencer devotes a chapter to the consideration of what he calls the most general forms into which the manifestations of the unknown are re-divisible; and these forms he finds to be these five: space, time, matter, motion, force.

"Now, if the starting point of religion is really scientific, it must follow that these five forms which are the factors of all phenomena ought to make their appearance at an early stage in her scheme. We shall not, of course, expect to find them expressed in the terminology of science, but shall look for their theological equivalents. Is this expectation realized? We answer, that in the first two verses (of Genesis) we shall find all five. They are these:

"In the beginning" . . . . Time
"God created the heavens". . . . . Space
"And the earth". . . . . Matter
"And the Spirit of Elohim" . . . . Force
"Moved". . . . . Motion."*

2. GEOLOGY, the science of the earth's structure and constitution, treating of the operation of its physical forces, and the past history of its developments, is one of the youngest of the sciences. Pythagoras and Strabo, the only men among the ancients whose scientific opinions deserve much notice, made scarcely a beginning in the direction of geology;

*"The Conflict of Truth," L. Hugh Capron, p. 135.

and Pythagoras belonged to the sixth century B. C., and Strabo to the first B. C. During the dark ages, no progress was made; but in the sixteenth century geological questions began to stir Italy, especially, the nature of fossils. In the seventeenth century Leibnitz and others carried on researches, but it was not till a full century later that Smith, in 1790, published his "Tabular View of the British Strata," the issue of his geological map of England, in 1815, forming an epoch in the history of this science, since which strides have been rapid.

A department of knowledge, thus first really explored in the eighteenth century, would, therefore, be most unlikely to prove in accord with the opening chapter of the earliest book of the Bible, if that were a merely human production. The correspondence, however, is remarkable.

Geology, so far as it may claim to have settled anything, outlines the story of creation somewhat thus:

First, a state of chaos or general confusion, the solid, liquid and fluid elements being mixed somewhat as they are in a great conflagration.

Secondly, that there was a light, chemical or cosmic in character, which pervaded this general chaos or confusion.

Thirdly, that condensation took place between

the steaming vapors above and below, those below forming rain and water, those above forming clouds, and occupying what is called the firmament. There came to be thus an "expanse" of atmosphere between the waters of the clouds and the waters of the sea.

Fourthly, that out of this great abyss of waters, the dry land appeared as the waters subsided.

Fifthly, that upon this continent thus arising above the waters, vegetation began to appear, and took three forms—plant, herb and tree, or the grasses, the plants and the trees.

Sixthly, animal life, beginning with what are known as the "protozoa" or first forms of life, which developed out of the ooze of the ocean bed; animal life ascending through its different grades until,

Seventhly, man comes on the scene as the consummate climax and crown of God's creative work.

Chaos, chemical light, expanse of atmosphere, appearance of land, vegetation in three forms, animal life, from the protozoa to the higher vertebrata, and, finally, man—exactly Moses' order in the first chapter of Genesis! First chaos; then God says, "Let light be," and light was; then an expanse of atmosphere, called in the English Bible, the firmament, but in the Hebrew "Rākyā"—an expanse—a marvellously accurate word; then the continent, the dry land; vegetation in three forms; and then life—"the waters brought forth life;" then, bye and bye, higher animals, and at the end of the mammalia, man himself.

Nothing was known about geology when Moses wrote, nor for thousands of years after. Who was it that guided him in this poetic description of Creation, to give thus accurately what the most modern of sciences affirms was the original order? There is nothing else like this in ancient literature. Whenever any of the ancient writers touched the science of creation absurd blunders were made. Even Plato thought the earth to be an intelligent being, and earthquakes were supposed to be such motions of the earth as a huge animal would make if writhing in pain!

In styling the description of creation as "poetic," it is not meant to give currency to the notion that these first chapters of Genesis are simply a poem, having no historic fact behind them. When Moses as a prophet was shown the vision of creation, he must have looked back, as John in the Apocalypse looked forward; and as a series of visions of creation passed before his mind, he described what he saw: an evening darkness, and a morning developing into light; another evening developing into another morning; and so another, and still another; until the six creative days all passed before him in this backward prophetic vision; and probably he did not understand what he himself wrote, as is said of the prophets (1 Peter 1:10–12), nor does any reader, however reverent and scientific, yet understand all that was then written; the studies of eternity alone will clothe these visions with their full celestial meaning. Meanwhile, those who search this Book reverently, find here and there suggestions from God to make them confident of His authorship of these mysterious pages.

3. The science of COMPARATIVE ANATOMY is only about one hundred years old. Cuvier, about the beginning of the nineteenth century, lifted what had hitherto been a mass of unconnected details to the dignity of a science. He compared the various forms of animal life, observing and recording points of similarity and dissimilarity; and so arranged facts according to a scientific classification. Comparative anatomy shows an order in the animal creation, from the lowest forms to the highest, rather than reversely, the question of rank among vertebrate animals being determined by the proportion of brain to the spinal column. In fish it is 2 to 1; in reptiles, 2½ to 1; in birds, 3 to 1; in mammals, 4 to 1; then in man it takes a leap, and the

proportion of brain to the spinal column is 33 to 1, which raises man far above any other animal.

Common sense and observation might have shown Moses that man is far above mammals as a class, and the mammals higher than most fishes and birds, but no common sense or ordinary observation would have shown that the fish belongs below the reptile, or the reptile below the bird. Yet, thousands of years before comparative anatomy took rank among the sciences, Moses followed the correct order of classification in this story of creation. A candid and rational scientist looking at that first chapter of Genesis, must ask how any unaided human mind could have guided the hand that wrote those words.

4. ANTHROPOLOGY is the science of man's constitution. The question arises as we look on mankind, "How is man made?" Was there any science in the days of Moses to teach him how man was constituted? Yet, in the second chapter of Genesis, with the boldness of certainty, he writes, that "God formed man out of the dust of the ground, and breathed into his nostrils the breath of life," (Hebrew, "the breath of lives"), as though this phrase included both the animal life man has in common with the animal creation, and the spiritual life he received in common with God.

The Bible and Science

According to the Word of God, man is a compound of spirit, soul, and body,* and, as taught in the twelfth chapter of Ecclesiastes, when "the dust returns to the earth as it was," "the spirit returns unto God who gave it," death being the dissolution and separation of that which God brought into original unity. That leaves little room for the theory of the "sleep of souls," for when one dies, he does not go into the earth, body and soul, to sleep there, but, while the dust returns to the earth, the spirit returns to God who gave it,—a plain reference to the original record in the second chapter of Genesis.

"God formed man out of the dust of the ground." The human body suggests little if any similarity in composition to the earth. Moses had no knowledge, as a human writer, that his body was one with the ground, but modern chemical analysis detects at least fourteen elements in the human body identical with the "dust,"—such as oxygen, hydrogen, nitrogen, silicon, magnesia, sodium, phosphorus, carbon. Yet nothing could be more unlike matter in its highly organized form in the human body, than the "dust" of the ground from which that human body is divinely declared to have been formed. It was reserved for modern

*1 Thes. v: 23.

analytical chemistry to demonstrate that what
Moses wrote is exactly true, when he represented
the Creator as taking the plain earth clay and
making out of that the human organism, though
nothing whatsoever in man's appearance suggests
this as a fact of observation. It has to be known
scientifically, yet it could not have been known
scientifically when Moses wrote Genesis.

In the story of the creation three words are used
that are similar, yet unlike, the difference being
more apparent in the Hebrew, though seen also in
the English—"created," "formed," "made." One
of these words means "to make, out and out";
another, "to form out of preëxisting matter," as a
potter takes clay and forms it into a vessel; and the
other means "to give a cosmical form," that is, to
make with reference to plan, symmetry, order,
beauty, as God took crude matter and formed it
into crystals.

No one of these expressions is used in connection with light. How unique are those five words
in the Hebrew, "Be light, and light was." It is
not recorded that God said, "Let earth be, and
earth was," or "Let stars be, and stars were."
But he said, "Let light be." Light is not a substance. There have been two modern theories of
light,—the corpuscular theory and the undulatory

theory; but the later discoveries have shown that light is a mode of motion,—vibrations so rapid through the ether that they pass over 186,000 miles a second. Why should not Moses have said that God "created" light, as he does say that He created the light bearers. He called forth the light. He made the celestial lamp or light-bearers out of material. He did not make the light out of material, new, or preëxisting; He simply bade it send through the universe vibrations like those of a musical chord. How majestic and magnificent! "In the beginning God;" "In the beginning God created;" "In the beginning God created the heavens and the earth;" "In the beginning God said, 'Be light,' and light was." He kept the sacred writers from the mistakes that mere observers would have made, and that they did make when they began to teach natural science. There was in Infinite Intelligence and Omniscience behind the ignorance of Moses, which guarded his pen from making any of those fatal mistakes that would have marred the Word of God through all the ages.

The 28th and 38th chapters of Job, two chapters in what is probably the oldest of all poems, have been declared to contain more science than the whole literature of the human race up to the Christian era, and some of the most remarkable anticipations of scientific discovery are to be found there.

Several great discoveries of modern times could not, in the nature of the case, have been known to any writers of the Bible; and yet the phraseology of the Bible is found in every case marvellously accommodated to them. The discoveries referred to are such as the following: The vast number of the stars and the immensity of space; the universal laws of motion and rotation, the nature and properties of light, and of lightning the weight of the atmosphere, and the circulation of the blood.

(1.) *The vast number of the stars*. This is entirely a modern discovery. The first reliable catalogue of the stars was made by Hipparchus, about 150 B. C., and the second by Ptolemy about 150 years after Christ. Both these catalogues give, in the entire southern and northern celestial hemispheres, about 3,000—a very easy number to count, and there was then no idea of any other stars invisible to the naked eye. When Galileo turned his telescope toward the heavens on the 7th of January, 1610, for the first time it was known that there were stars never before seen; he saw the four satellites of Jupiter, and announced his remarkable discovery. From this point, as telescopes improved, discovery went forward until now it is known that the stars are absolutely countless. When the elder Herschel erected his monster telescope, forty feet in length, and turned it to the heavens in 1789, he talked of "star dust." He threw new light on the Milky Way and the constitution of nebulæ, and, in fact, was the first to give to the human mind any conception of the immensity of the universe. He found that what appeared to be dust on the surface of the firmament, was simply groups of stars so thickly crowded that they could not be distinguished by the naked eye. When Lord Rosse mounted his giant reflector, weighing twelve tons, in his park at Parsonstown, in 1845, within the range of its speculum, he computed that about four hundred millions might be rendered visible, and yet that was only the third great stage in discovery of their innumerable multitude.*

The Milky Way, floating its white banner across the firmament, is a vast host of stars seen edgewise, stretching away into infinite space, and nobody can trace that to its limit; our little solar system

*As to the number of stars, Herschel computed that in one hour 116,000 passed over the field of his telescope. Up to the sixth and seventh magnitude, they number 14,000, but beyond that, are countless multitudes only revealed by most powerful telescopes, and others that photography reveals, too far off to be seen even by the telescopic eye, and whose rays as they now reach our eye, started on their journey long before we were born, perhaps thousands of years ago.

is but an atom in what Mr. Proctor calls, "the luminous sand of the Milky Way." It is, therefore, literally true that the stars are countless.

This is a notable modern discovery, first hinted at by Galileo; yet the Bible anticipated it as far back as the time of Abraham. When God appeared to him and gave him the great covenant promise, he told him that his seed should be ultimately as numerous as the "dust of the earth" and the "stars of the sky." There must have seemed to Abraham a great difference between the number of the stars and the number of the atoms of dust, yet they are alike countless. God knew these facts when He told him that his terrestrial seed should be as numerous as the dust, and his celestial seed as numerous as the stars. But it was reserved for remote generations to find that both comparisons are equally apt. So Jeremiah wrote (XXIII:22), "As the hosts of heaven cannot be numbered, neither the sand of the sea measured,"—comparing the host of stars to the grains of sand on the sea shore. The language of the Holy Scriptures is thus exactly adapted to facts not then known, but as unfolded by recent astronomical investigation. The enigmatic expressions of the Old Testament waited for a score of centuries for a scientific interpreter.

52

The Bible and Science

(2.) *The Immensity of space*. Of this the ancients had no idea. They supposed the earth to be stationary, and the whole of the celestial bodies to move around it once in every twenty-four hours; and that the "firmament" was a firm or solid sphere as of metal, and the stars, points of light, or lamps, hung in the concave as in a dome; they had no conception of these immeasurable, inconceivable dimensions and distances.

It began to be noted, however, that as some of the stars were fixed,—did not change their relative position, notwithstanding the change of position of the earth in its orbit—they must be at immense distances. The earth being about ninety millions of miles from the sun, has an orbit of some hundred and eighty millions of miles diameter. Even the modern era of the telescope only began to reveal the immensity of space. Some further conception of it is furnished in the fact that the unit of measurement, as to the distances of the stars, is the velocity of light. Light moves 186,000 miles a second; yet even that is too small for a unit of measurement; astronomers have to take for this purpose the distance over which light travels in a year, or over 60,000 times the distance of the earth from the sun. That is the unit of measurement, so it is customary to say that *a*

Centaurus is four years off as light travels, Arcturus, 25 years off, Polaris, 46 years off, and Canopus, 108.

Yet even this immensity of space is similarly anticipated in the Word of God! For example, Jeremiah says (XXXI: 37), "If the heavens above can be measured, and the foundations searched out beneath, I will also cast off the seed of Israel." He used the boundless immensity of space as the argument for God's boundless fidelity to His people. When man can measure the heavens above, then will God's care for Israel as His beloved people find its limit. Here the immeasurable spaces of the heavens are assumed. So, in the 55th chapter of Isaiah, verse 9, it is said, "As the heavens are higher than the earth, so are My ways higher than your ways, and My thoughts than your thoughts;" that is to say, the infinite height of heaven above the earth becomes the symbol of the infinite height of God's grace above the deserts of man. Again, in Psalm CIII: 11, "As the heaven is high above the earth, so great is His mercy toward them that fear Him. As far as the east is from the west, so far hath He removed our transgressions from us." The writer of the 103rd Psalm himself had no conception of what is known by us—that go as far as you will to the east there is still an east, and as far as you will to the west, there is still a west; but God who spoke through him knew that only when you can measure the distance between the remotest east and west can you measure how far away from the forgiven sinner God has removed his sins,—astronomical infinities are brought in to illustrate the infinity of the love and grace of God! There is no accident about that! It is manifestly intelligent design.

(3.) The Universal *Law of Motion* is a difficult subject to touch upon in a brief space. No discovery of modern times has been, in some respects, more startling. Science constructs a sort of vibratory ladder according to the number of vibrations per second, running from sixteen and a half up to 480,000,000,000—those of the violet ray of light.

Beginning at the lowest audible note and going up eleven octaves, the limits of sound are reached at 38,000 vibrations to the second. Then, passing an unknown region, electricity is reached with about one hundred million vibrations; then dark heat, about 130 thousand million vibrations; then comes the octave of colour, corresponding to the octave of sound, the red rays with about 400 thousand millions and so on up the spectrum to violet with 480 thousand millions. These vibrations, it is claimed, have been at least approximately reckoned or calculated. Thus not only sound is found to be the result of vibration, but likewise electricity and heat, colour and light. The ear does not detect colour, as it does sound, because the auditory nerve is less sensitive and delicate than the optical. Light really sings, only our ears are not attuned to its melodies and harmonies; we do not hear but see it. But light and sound are closely akin, both of the same nature, both produced by vibrations such as those of the chords of a musical instrument. Bible language singularly anticipates even this discovery. In Job XXXVIII:7 we read that "the morning stars sang together,"—"gave forth vibrations," like a musical instrument, as the Hebrew word literally means. Again, in Psalm LXV: 8, "Thou makest the outgoings of the morning and evening (sunrise and sunset) to give forth vibrations." The translators rendered it "rejoice," but the fact is that Nature, like a great orchestra, gives forth vibrations in different notes and chords of colour, which peal into the ears of the Lord God of Hosts; every morning sunrise and every evening sunset are as choral anthems in His ears! and they would be so in ours if our ears were delicate enough, as perhaps they will be, in the body of glory, in the future life, to detect this "music of the spheres."

The Bible and Science

The poetic language of Holy Scripture thus again anticipates or forecasts one of the most recent and striking of all modern discoveries. To such scientific facts is adapted the language of the 19th Psalm, verses 1-3. "The heavens declare (or speak forth) the glory of God. Day uttereth speech unto day, and night showeth knowledge unto night." "There is no speech or language where their voice is not heard," etc. The psalmist is describing the sun, moon and stars in the heavens, and their radiations of light, in the language of song and anthem, speech and conversation. God knew from all eternity that light and sound were akin, and it is natural that He should so guide the writers of the Bible that their words should accommodate themselves to all these marvels of scientific fact not to be known for milleniums afterward.

4. The *Refraction of Light* is another discovery, comparatively modern. Ptolemy, the astronomer, is credited with the first intimation of it. Refraction is the bending of the ray out of its direct course as it meets different media of transmission. If the sun's rays were not thus refracted, only the direct or perpendicular rays would reach the earth, the others glancing off and being reflected into space, so that man would get little benefit; but the

atmosphere surrounds the earth in strata or layers, and when the indirect rays encounter these at an angle they are caught and bent round, like the fingers of the hand, and so retained for use. That also seems forecast in the Bible.

In the 38th chapter of Job, verses 12 and 13, we read: "Hast Thou commanded the morning since Thy days, and caused the dayspring to know his place." The original suggests the idea of "coming up to his post in time," which is true to fact, for the diurnal rotation of the earth on its axis is so regular that the day dawn "has not varied the one-thousandth of a second, from the exact time due, for the last two thousand years." Then follow these words: "That it might *take hold of the ends* of the earth," literally bend round like the fingers, and so lay hold—poetic phraseology, but containing within itself all the suggestion of the scientific truth of refraction.

(5.) *The Weight of the Atmosphere*. The discovery of the law of gravitation has been comparatively recent, but it was supposed, even after this force began to be suspected, that certain substances, such as those that we call etherial and volatile, were not affected by it. Newton demonstrated that its action is universal. Galileo, before him, had found reason to believe the atmosphere to

58

have weight, or gravity, but the thought had never
dawned on the mind of the ancients, and no hint of
it is found in Plato, Aristotle, or other philosophers
of old time. In the Bible it is boldly stated, that
it is a part of God's administration "to make the
weight for the winds" (Job xxviii:35), literally, to
"balance the winds"—exactly the fact—for by
their weight they help to keep in equilibrium the
great scales of the universe.* Thus, unknown to the
ancients—undreamed of by their wise men—this
fact is definitely affirmed in the mystic language of
this old poem.

(6.) *The Circulation of the blood*, discovered by
William Harvey, in 1619, is, therefore, a very recent
discovery. Certain rudimental facts about this
system of circulation every school boy understands,
such as that there are practically two hearts, each
having two parts; and that the auricles receive the
blood from the veins, and the ventricles pulse the
blood through the arteries. When the blood,
forced out through the arteries, deposits its nutri-
ment, it is drawn back through the veins, to be
reinvigorated in the lungs. Thus one part of the
heart is of the nature of a fountain or spring; but,
there being no pulsation in the veins, the other

*The weight of the atmosphere is found to be 14.73 lbs. to the
square inch, and the total weight of the air, 11.67085 trillion lbs., or
1-188,000,000th of the entire weight of the globe.

part is a receptacle—a cistern rather than a fountain—a reservoir for the reception of venous blood.

Again, the lung is somewhat like a "pitcher," and the tube by which air enters it is like the spout of a pitcher. The lung is closely connected with the heart's cistern, and a great conduit carries the blood from the lung to the auricles.

In Ecclesiastes xii : 6, 7, the substance of this great discovery is hinted mysteriously by Solomon: "Or ever the silver cord be loosed, or the golden bowl be broken, or the pitcher be broken at the fountain, or the wheel broken at the cistern." What this means, we are told: "Then shall the dust return to the earth as it was, and the spirit shall return unto God Who gave it." These are four poetic descriptions of death. Life is a kind of quadruped, moving on four legs: the energy of the brain, the nervous system—cerebro-spinal and sympathetic; and the lung and heart systems, with their great mysteries of respiration and circulation.

"Or the wheel broken at the cistern." In the East to this day are wells where a wheel pumps up the water through one pipe to discharge it through another. This is what the heart does, pumping up the blood through pipes of blue, to propel it through pipes of red, and long before William

Harvey dreamed of the circulation of the blood, God inspired Solomon to use language which not only suggests the general facts of the heart's action but hints the two parts of the organ, the "fountain" and the "cistern," the ventricles and auricles. William Harvey himself might have coveted this inspired description as a poetic statement of the facts he made known to the human race.

(7.) *The Universal Law of Rotation.* The diurnal rotation of the earth, already referred to, in passing, was not known to the ancients, who thought it a stationary body. Yet we read, for instance, "It is turned as clay to the seal, and stands like an embroidered garment." (Job XXXVIII: 14.) The reference is to the cylindrical seal, which revolved somewhat as, in a printing machine, the cylinder that holds the type and the cylinder that holds the paper roll over each other, and so the paper takes the impression of the type, and stands forth in more or less beautiful forms. So the earth is revolved as the clay under the seal, and takes the impression of the light and heat and appears like an embroidered garment. If this be the meaning of this rather obscure figure in Job, it suggests, thousands of years before this was known, the diurnal rotation of the earth. Moreover, all these stars and suns are moving. As the earth revolves

God's Living Oracles

on its axis every day, and in its orbit around the sun, once in 365 days, so the sun has its own axial rotation and its own orbit of revolution. But it was reserved for modern times to prove that in a similar manner the whole of the visible universe is in motion, all heavenly bodies circling about their respective centers and the universe as a whole through its orbit in incredibly long periods of time. Mädler believed he had discovered the universal center, in the star Alcyone, in the little group of seven, called the Pleiades, and suggested that this star might be the throne of God.

In the 38th chapter of Job, we read: "Canst thou bind the sweet influences of Pleiades?" The Pleiades were so called from "pleo," to sail, because the rising of this constellation brought spring rains, but the Chaldaic word means a "hinge," a "pivot," an "axle," the word meaning what moves itself and moves everything else with it. Here the language is accommodated to the fact of universal rotation and suggests that the Pleiades form at least one of the hinges, pivots or axles for this universal motion.

(8.) *The Nature, Properties and uses of Lightning.* For thousands of years lightning was to man nothing but a disastrous mystery accompanying violent storms and often doing immense damage.

The Bible and Science

It was reserved for Benjamin Franklin to follow out the lines of previous experimental investigation, until he proved that lightning could be laid hold of and utilized. His experiment with his kite, bristling with points, which he flew in the thunder storm, showed that this mysterious force, conducted down the string and gathered in the key at the end, passed with a spark and a slight shock into his knuckle; and so was suggested to him the device of the lightning rod, drawing down the wrath of heaven and turning it harmlessly into the earth, so often used in illustration of the work of the Lord Jesus Christ in Redemption. To that great discovery, we owe it that, in the twentieth century, lightning has become a motor, a messenger, an illuminator, and is fast becoming also a therapeutic agent for the discovery and remedy of disease.

The discoveries in electricity since Franklin's day have come with such rapidity that they seem to surpass any previous unveiling of scientific truth. They constitute the wonder of the ages, and no one can tell what the next few years may develop in electrical science.

But the ancients knew nothing about the lightning flash, which seemed capricious and lawless—it came, they knew not whence, and went, they knew not whither; the lightning suddenly appeared in connection with the storm, then vanished as suddenly as it came; it was impossible to trace it to its dwelling place or determine anything about its philosophy. Man has now found that he can summon the lightning and bid it go on his errands; that he can make it flash intelligence to the earth's ends; that he can control the artillery of heaven, draw down the volleys of destruction and make them the means of construction—his servants on the earth; that he can cause the lightning, which once destroyed and killed, to heal and make alive,—in fact, totally turning about this most destructive agent of the universe.

Even this is forecast in the Holy Scripture! Look again to the 38th chapter of Job. Here in this old poem arises one of those lofty peaks of inspiration where God seems to set aside human instrumentality, and Himself appears as the speaker:* "Canst thou commission the lightnings that they may come and say to thee, Here we are? Canst thou inspire them with intelligence? Canst

* Compare Mrs. Helen M. Spurrell's scholarly translation of the Old Testament, published by James Nisbet & Co., London, for which there was so little sale that the edition was sent to the paper-mill, and a copy can be found only in some secondhand book shop. No translation perhaps surpasses it in suggestiveness.

thou give them understanding to obey thy behests?"*

Other great discoveries are similarly anticipated in Scripture. For example, the correlation and conservation of force.

Such expressions as these are found side by side with others: "He hangeth the earth upon nothing," when no one had suspected as yet that so balanced are the great correlative forces of the universe, centrifugal and centripetal, that the earth is hung in space upon nothing, and has no foundations; its pillars are set in no sockets, because God has so arranged the invisible and silent working forces that they keep the whole universe in a state of equipoise.

While men are assaulting this Book of God, and speaking in terms, sometimes unmeasured, of what they call its errors and its absurdities, all the material worlds and forces of the universe stand as a great orchestra, pealing forth their anthem to Him, Who, in His infinite love and grace, gave such a revelation of His will to the sons of men! "In His temple doth every whit shout, glory!"†

* Job xxxviii: 35. (Hebrew.)　　† Psalm xxix: 9 (Hebrew).

CHAPTER IV

THE BIBLE AND PREDICTION

THE first great moral question which demands an intelligent answer is this: Is there a God? and the second is like unto it: Is this God's book? Has God spoken to man? No questions can transcend in importance these two, for they form the basis of all spiritual and religious thought and inquiry.

It has been already conceded that the presumption is against the Bible as a divine book. The fact that other books have also claimed to be a supernatural product throws the burden of proof on the Bible itself and its defenders; and this is conceded in the challenge for investigation and in the treatment accorded to honest doubt as perfectly legitimate; but the Bible's challenge is a fearless one, for it confronts every questioner with evidence that ought to satisfy, and will satisfy, all sincere inquirers after truth. Prediction furnishes a burden of evidence that must stagger any unbeliever, this department of evidence so abounding with proofs, found in the Word of God, itself, as to make honest doubt impossible.

The Bible and Prediction

As this book claims to be a royal message, issued to God's human subjects, it is of the highest consequence that as such it should be accompanied and authenticated by His royal signature and seal. Moreover, in accordance with the importance of the proclamation and the gravity of the crisis, is the importance that such signature and seal should be obviously affixed to the document, so that all whom it concerns may be satisfied that it issues from the King. Because the Bible claims to be God's word to man, and to treat of the most serious subjects that can claim our consideration, it is correspondingly necessary that its authentication should be absolutely beyond a reasonable doubt, otherwise it would be unreasonable to believe in and accept it. A supernatural book must have supernatural attestation; the work must show the skilled workman, and be worthy of him; not a botch and a blunder, or a tissue of absurdities, but such as might be expected of its great Author. An enlightened mind honours the bible by demanding such proof. Locke, in his essay on "The Human Understanding," well says, "to abandon the use of reason in matters of revelation is like putting out the eyes in order to use the telescope."

There are two conspicuous methods, both supernatural, by which the bible claims to be attested: one is prophecy and the other is miracle. A prophecy—using the word now in the sense of supernatural prediction—is a miracle of word or utterance; a miracle is a supernatural work or performance: and each of them reveals God. A prediction reveals Omniscience, a miracle reveals Omnipotence, both of which are divine attributes; and, therefore, prophecy and miracle are fitting modes of attesting a divine document.

It remains now to be proven that these methods of attestation have actually accompanied this book, and thus demonstrate that it is a supernatural revelation.

Prediction has a special value as appealing to the rational powers, even of the unbelieving. Some other forms of attestation can be appreciated only by the believer, the Bible being something like a cathedral, whose richest beauties can be seen only from within. To understand the stained glass windows of such an architectural monument, it is needful to look at them from the inside, with the sunlight shining through them. But there are other beauties of the cathedral that may be seen from without. Prophecy is intended to call the attention of the reasoning mind to the magnificent and majestic proportions of the Bible, not only as seen from within but from without. Then, by first convincing the reader of its divine inspiration, it prepares him to enter within as a believer and see other beauties as of stained glass windows, imperial columns, and groined arches.

Prophecy, again, is of special value because it is permanent in its witness. Miracles which belong to a remote age were especially designed to lay foundations for the Christian faith; when such foundations were laid, these particular miraculous attestations would naturally cease in history. If repeated in subsequent ages, their frequency would imply diminution of their force, since the power of a miracle largely lies in the fact that it is extraordinary—an interruption of the ordinary natural process, and, if occurring too often, could, of course, no longer attract attention by its novelty and startling character.

Prophecy, however, is a perpetual miracle. While other miracles lose force in proportion as the time of their occurrence is remote, prophecy increases in force as the interval is the more extended between the prediction and its fulfilment. It is a significant fact that God should have put predictive prophecy as a seal upon His Word, so that any candid doubter, seeking for light, might find it; and so God perpetuates the evidence through the ages. While the multiplicity and remoteness of miracles would decrease their force, the multiplicity and remoteness of predictions increases theirs.

It has already been claimed that no rational, sensible and candid mind can examine the evidence from prophecy, and yet account for the Bible as a merely human production. Why, then, is there so much doubt? First, because there is so much ignorance, and some of it wilful. Here is this book, containing within itself every necessary attestation of its divine character. Yet how large a portion even of the more intelligent classes spend more time on the daily newspaper than they do on the Word of God! Fictitious literature floods the market, and two-thirds of the books drawn from public libraries are said to be novels, which shows the trend of modern reading. How seldom is any proportionate and discriminating attention given to this divine Book. There would be few skeptics on the earth if this Bible were read as other literature is.

Some who do not entirely neglect this book resort to evasive ways of interpreting its mysteries, such as the poetic method, which sometimes means denying all literal interpretation, and evaporating predictions into vague and indefinite general statements. Some even venture to explain these predictions as shrewd conjectures, and their remarkable fulfilments as results of fortunate guesses; or they compare them to the forecasts of the weather prophet, who, having the records of the weather for many years previous, and carefully observing the phenomena of the present, is able sagaciously to predict to-morrow's atmosphere and cloudland. Examination will show how utterly unsatisfactory and untenable such explanations are, and that they all betray a lack of careful and conscientious examination of the subject.

Biblical predictions have been fulfilled in history, and some of them in the history of our own times. They cannot be dismissed as ambiguous, "with double sense deluding," like the ancient Delphic oracles, for nothing is more clear and unmistakable than the statements found in the Word of God as to future events. These introductory remarks will be vindicated and illustrated as the investigation proceeds.

One remarkable fact is that God has not only attested prediction by fulfilling it historically, but has often used professed skeptics to *record* such fulfilments. Out of the mouths of enemies of the Christian religion have come some of the main confirmations and attestations of the accuracy of

biblical predictions! Volney, an infidel, who held
the human origin and essential falsity of all
religious systems, and scouted all idea of a supernatural revelation, has left on record some of the
most accurate observations of facts, verifying
many prophecies of Holy Scriptures. He went to
oriental lands, described what he saw accurately
and carefully and, taking views of ruins, became a
sort of photographer of prophecy;* and Gibbon, the
infidel historian, has contributed scores of pages
to similar confirmation of the word of God, all
unconsciously and unmeaningly on his part. God
also took the sun as His coworker and cowitness.
The daguerreotype, invented early in the last
century, has enabled many who cannot travel to
foreign lands, to behold the remarkable fulfilments
of prediction, brought near by the magic art of the
camera, the sunlight reproducing those scenes of
desolation which prove that God's word has been
fulfilled.

We are bidden to search the Scriptures whether
these things are so. In the prophecy of Isaiah
(xxxiv:16) is a notable challenge: "Seek ye out
of the book of the Lord, and read; no one of these
shall fail, none shall want her mate: for my mouth
it hath commanded, and his spirit it hath gathered

---

* Volney s " Ruins," published 1794.

them." This is ordinarily taken to refer to those
animals of which the prophet had been speaking,
that in the desert of Idumea should hide among its
ruins, each one calling to its mate. But another
rendering and reference have been suggested:
"Search ye in the writings of Jehovah, and read.
Not one of all these (His sayings) shall stand alone;
not one (prediction) shall lack its counterpart (in
fulfilment). For the mouth of Jehovah hath
given (the decree), and His spirit it hath brought
(prediction and fulfilment) together."

Such is God's injunction, that the reader shall
search out the words of Jehovah, as to coming
events, and read, and then show one prediction
that has not been fulfilled, save only such as may
concern events yet future. Not one such prediction stands alone,—not one fails of its mate or
counterpart, in the historic events.

Can such coincidence be accounted for on the
law of probabilities? Is it possible that these
predictions have simply come true by accident?
The law of simple and compound probability is
familiar to those who know the common principles
of mathematics. A single prediction made, concerning future events, may or may not prove
accurate; hence simple probability represents the
chance of its coming to pass by the fraction, one-

half, or one chance in two. For instance, if it were predicted that this will be a year of marine disasters, the prediction has a half chance of accomplishment. But if it be added that these marine disasters will be in the Atlantic Ocean, as each item can have at most only its half chance, we are in the realm of compound probability, and must multiply one-half by itself, which gives us one-quarter chance. If another item be added, that these disasters are to be in February, we have at best one chance in eight; and so on, as each new particular is added, multiplying again by one-half.

In the prophecies about Tyre, Philistia, Babylon, Nineveh, Egypt, etc., there is an average of forty different details in each case, so that one-half must be raised to its corresponding power to express the insignificant fraction of probability that so many particulars will be realized in any one event. The numerator will be one, with a denominator of hundreds of millions. It is needful only to make such a simple calculation in arithmetic, to know that these things could not come to pass by a mere accident. To attempt to throw discredit upon such a body of prediction, shows either the stupidity of the fool or the trickery of the knave.

In applying criteria by which to test prophecy, the more severe the better, that there may be no room for doubt on the part of any candid inquirer. There are four such criteria, but the test will be still more decisive if we add a fifth.

First, Remoteness of Time. In order that there shall be no possibility of any efficient agency on the part of him who predicts the event, in bringing it to pass, there must be such separation between the prediction and the fulfilment that the prophet can have no power, directly or indirectly, to influence the result.

Secondly. Minuteness of Detail. The particulars of the prophecy should be so many and minute that there shall be no possibility of accounting by shrewd guess-work for the accuracy of the fulfilment.

Thirdly. Novelty of Combination. There should have been nothing in previous history which makes it possible to forecast a like event in the future. There must be something new in the combination; something fresh, startling and original in the prediction and the method of its fulfilment, to prove divine intervention.

Fourthly. Mystery of Contradiction. That is to say, when the prophecy is examined carefully, it shall present such paradoxes or apparent contradictions, that it is impossible to understand the prophecy fully until the events have supplied the key to its mysteries.

Fifthly.   Clearness of Forecast—that there shall be such perspicuity of statement as not to be ambiguous, but obvious in its general meaning; and that especially, when the event occurs, it shall be seen to correspond without question to the original prediction.

These are confessedly severe tests, and yet by them every prophecy of the Holy Scripture may be tried and not fail.   Prediction finds its mate— the historic event; there is close correspondence between the forecast and the fulfilment.

We turn attention, first, to certain prophecies of the Bible which center or cluster about the Jews; noting in advance, that this is true of most predictions.   We may put in the center of the whole prophetic scheme, the word "Israel," for even the few predictions which have to do with the world kingdoms are not disconnected with God's chosen people—the Jews.   The uniqueness of the scheme of prophecy is found partly in this unity: it does not consist of scattered fragments without system, but Israel stands as its crystallizing center.

On the southwest of Judea, lay Egypt and Arabia; on the southeast, Moab, Ammon and Edom or Idumea; on the east and northeast,

The Bible and Prediction

Babylon and Nineveh, on the north and west, Philistia and Samaria; and on the northwest, Tyre and Sidon and Phoenicia.

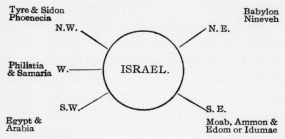

Thus Israel holds the center, with from ten to twelve nations ranged around. The offence of each of these nations was different and so was God's method of dealing with them. They all fell under His curse because of something that they had done toward Israel: Egypt keeping Israel in slavery; Philistia drawing off her strength and harassing her from the western border; Edom and Moab and Ammon interfering with her entrance into or progress in the land of promise, delighting in her destruction and decay; Babylon and Nineveh were the lands of captivity; Tyre and Sidon, responsible for the introduction of the worship of Baal into Israel and Judah.

God's punishment was "poetic retribution." As the rhyme and rhythm of one line correspond

with those of another, in versification, so, in their
punishment there was such correspondence between
the offence committed and the penalty exacted
as showed that they were matched the one against
the other, as when Haman swung from the very
gallows that he built for Mordecai.

Brevity forbids extensive quotations from the
predictions written by Ezekiel, Jeremiah, Nahum,
Joel, Daniel, Isaiah, and others, concerning these
nations, which occupy scores of chapters.

From the prophecies about Egypt two or three
predictions may be chosen as a key to the rest;
they occupy the 29th, 30th, 31st, and 32nd chapters of Ezekiel. A few expressions occurring here
are very striking: Egypt "shall be the basest of
the kingdoms . . . They shall no more rule
over the nations." (Ezek. xxix: 15.) "I will
make the river dry . . . I will make the land
waste, and all that is therein, by the hand of
strangers." (xxx:12.) And further in the 13th
verse: ". . . and there shall be no more a
prince of the land of Egypt." Here are a few
among scores of particulars: Egypt, the largest,
most distinguished and most exalted of ancient
kingdoms was to become the basest; the Nile
Valley, which made it the granary of the world,
was to become dry and desert; where for two thou-

sand years there had been a succession of native princes, there was to be no more a prince of its own land. What was more impossible, according to human conjecture? The most enduring monuments on earth had been erected by the Egyptians —witness those artificial mountains, the pyramids; and yet this kingdom that once led the nations of the world, that had the most ancient and most distinguished dynasty, is even now before our eyes the basest of empires. The Nile Valley was the granary of the world; to-day its ancient bed is dry and eighty miles from the present channel, and another of the former beds is nothing but a sand heap, and the sand has drifted over that formerly fertile land until it has threatened to engulf the pyramids.

The story of the Mamelukes that reigned in Egypt is a remarkable bit of historical fact. About the middle of the thirteenth century (1240), these Mamelukes were brought over by the Sultan into Egypt, a band of twelve thousand military warriors trained for arms. Four years afterward, they rebelled; they assassinated the Sultan and elected one of their own number to occupy the Egyptian throne. Even then the succession did not follow in the line of the reigning sovereign, but when he died or was displaced, another slave from a fresh batch brought from Circassia was elected to the throne. There was not a ruler from the native princes of Egypt; and although, when the country was overrun by the Turks (1517), the sceptre passed nominally from these Mamelukes, they continued as Egyptian Beys until 1811, when the final blow was struck that demolished their power.

This was poetic retribution, indeed, and could only be traced to the Lord God of Recompenses Who shall surely requite. Egypt had reduced the Israelites to slavery and compelled them to serve rigorously in bondage, and possibly they were the builders of those imperishable pyramids. How did the God of Recompenses requite Egypt? For three hundred years He gave up this country that enslaved His own people, to be governed by slaves, so that there was no more a prince of the land of Egypt—another example of predictions which do not stand alone, but find their companion fulfilments, their counterpart in historic events.

In the prophecies about Philistia two or three features are prominent: (1). Ascalon, the great fortress, should be despoiled and destroyed, and be absolutely without inhabitant; (2) Ashdod, that resisted the longest of sieges (29 years), should be despoiled. Ascalon is uninhabited, although the ruins offer a good shelter from the storms of sand and rain with which the Mediterranean coast abounds. Just outside Ascalon is a mud village of the Fellaheen, who, when asked why they did not seek a refuge there, said they believed genii and spirits inhabit the ruins, and they dared not go and live there. And so this great fortress is not only despoiled, but remains literally without inhabitant.*

As to Tyre,—there was both an insular and a continental city by this name. The former stood on an island in the Mediterranean, half a mile or so from shore, compassed by impregnable walls washed by the sea at their base. This queen city of the Mediterranean could not be taken, as it was supposed. When Alexander followed Nebuchadnezzar in assault upon it, (332, B.C.), enraged that this island stronghold so withstood his power, he built out a mole from the mainland, turning the island into a peninsula. He scraped the ruins from the site of the continental city and carried them into the midst of the sea, in order to accomplish his purpose. Both cities have been destroyed, and exactly as the prophet said, what is left is "a rock for fishers to spread their nets upon."† When Dr. Alexander Keith visited these sites, and sought

*Zeph. ii: 1–7; Zech. ix: 1–8, etc.
† Jerem. xxv, xxvii; Ezek. xxvi–xxviii; Amos i: 9–15; Zech. ix: 2–4.

a place where he might pitch his tent, he found this mole as smooth as a rock, and the fishermen at that very time spreading their nets upon it to dry, and he took a photograph of it which he has reproduced in his exhaustive treatise on prophecy.

Herodotus says of Babylon that it had walls three hundred feet high, and seventy-five feet broad, so that three carriages could be driven abreast. There were eight miles of length between the river gates, the city standing over the bed of the Euphrates. Cyrus dug a great trench around the city, ostensibly as a bulwark for defense, but really to turn the waters into a new channel; and then, having successfully accomplished this engineering feat, exactly as was predicted, on a night of revelry, when the Babylonians were occupied with their own merriment, thinking their city impregnable, Cyrus and his army entered, advancing through the bed of the river, and from both ends of the channel at once. If, even then, those brazen gates had been closed, his army, caught in a trap, might have been destroyed; but this failed to be done and in their wild mirth the inhabitants were entirely unprepared to meet the foe. The prophecy (Jer. LI: 31): "Posts shall run to and fro to inform the king in his palace that the city is taken at each end," was literally fulfilled when, almost simultaneously, the army advanced into the city from each end of this river bed, and the posts, starting from both sides, encountered each other midway as they ran toward the king's palace. The dismayed people acted like cowards, even the king himself, locked up in his palace, voluntarily opening the doors. God had said: "I will open before him (Cyrus) the two-leaved gates," (of the palace) as He had also said, "The gates shall not be shut" (the brazen river gates).

Another prediction about Babylon was: "Two things shall come to thee in a moment, in one day, the loss of children and widowhood."* In the midst of the siege, so determined were they not to be driven to extremities by famine, that they strangled fifty thousand of their women and children, reserving only sufficient to bake bread to carry them through the siege; so that in one day, and as in one moment, the loss of children and widowhood came upon them, and there is nothing parallel to this in the history of mankind.

Thus prediction is fulfilled as it concerns that group of nations of which the Jews are the center, Egypt, Babylon and Assyria; Edom, Moab and Ammon; Tyre, Sidon and Phoenicia. Egypt that reduced Israel to slavery, was punished by becom-

* Isa. xlvii:9.

ing the basest of kingdoms, ruled over, about as long as the Israelites were held in bondage, by a race of Circassian slaves. Nineveh and Babylon, the lands of captivity, were to be destroyed, even their site unknown for many centuries. God said He would make Nineveh as a grave, and the great mounds rise on its site like huge graves in a deserted cemetery. Babylon was to be destroyed by the drying up of the Euphrates, and Nineveh by the inundation of the Tigris. There seemed no reason why these decrees should not have been reversed, Babylon's stream overflowing, and Nineveh's river drying up, but all took place as announced years before.

Edom, Ammon and Moab harassed Israel on her border by wars and incursions, and by the seduction to impurity, and their punishment was to be without inhabitant. Even the Rock City, whose sculptured temples and strongholds, cut into the solid bedrock, still exhibit marvels in comparison with which even St. Peter's Cathedral at Rome is a minor achievement—even Petra, exactly according to the decrees of prophecy, is inhabited only by the wild beasts specified in the predictions.

As to Tyre and Sidon, that entangled Israel as well as Judah in Baal and Astarte worship, not only is Tyre like a "rock for fishermen to spread their nets upon," but the temples and idols of Tyre and Sidon have no representative worshippers. Here, again, are startling prophecies fulfilled to the letter, but we have as yet touched only on the outskirts of this great theme.

The imperial seal of Almighty God is upon His Book. It fills the believer with awe, when he sees that this book has thus upon it the stamp of its Divine Author—the mark of heaven—the impress of eternity. Doubt and indifference can be explained only by the fact of moral depravity. The ruins of Egypt, of Babylon, of Tyre, of Nineveh, all typify this sadder ruin of humanity. The rejection of the Word of God is due more to the heart than to the head. Compelled to confront such a mass of overwhelming evidence, there are those who shut their eyes to the glory that beams from these pages as from the very throne of God,* that they may continue in sin. They deny the inspiration of the Bible because they find it impossible to believe and accept it as an inspired revelation, and yet to go on comfortably in evil-doing.† First men do violence to conscience, and then make shipwreck of faith. Were there no sin in the world, there would be no skepticism. But the time is coming, in the final assizes of the universe,

*Revelation v: 1-5.　　　　†I Timothy 1:19.

85

when the solemn question will be substantially asked: "What hast thou to say why sentence should not be pronounced upon thee according to law?" and it will be terrible in that day to be "speechless." God challenges all men to search His Book, to read and examine, to see whether His forecasts stand alone, unaccompanied by fulfilment; to observe how prophecy finds its mate in history, its counterpart in subsequent events; and so learn that it is because both the utterances of prophecy and the occurrences of history emanate from the same divine Mind, and obey the same decree of His inspiring spirit, that the predictive Word of God, and the providential Work of God, move together in such mystic eternal harmony.

CHAPTER V

THE BIBLE AND PREDICTION—Continued

THE prophecies of Christ—the great body of Messianic prediction—are reserved for separate treatment. Before entering upon these, other departments of prophecy need, and are entitled to, special investigation, as constituting in themselves phenomena of a remarkable character.

First, there are important predictions concerning the Jews themselves—the center of the general prophetic scheme. As God's chosen people, they have an important relation to the history of the race, and an important destiny in connection with it. God therefore decreed that, while severely punished and chastened for their idolatries and apostacies, they should, as a people, be preserved and ultimately restored to His favour (Romans XI). The 28th chapter of Deuteronomy is a comprehensive outline of prophecies about the Hebrew nation, containing no less than seventy particulars, most of which have already been exactly fulfilled; and others, referring to the final restoration of the Jews to their own land, and their re-

habilitation as a people, await future development, but, even now, seem fast approaching the
period of their accomplishment.

Seven marked predictions might be selected
from those which are on record about the Jews;

1. They would be so sorely besieged by enemies,
that women would devour their own children—
fulfilled in the sieges of Jerusalem, both under
Neubuchadnezzar, and under Titus.

2. They would be rooted out of their land and
carried afar into captivity,—fulfilled in the Baby-
lonian and Assyrian captivities, but forecast, in
part, in previous minor captivities, as related in
the book of Judges.

3. They were not to find rest in any of the lands
of their captivity, but be scattered abroad and
driven hither and thither as wanderers among all
nations.

4. They were to be despoiled by their enemies
and made a prey. So they have been in every
land where they have dwelt; and if, as in Great
Britain and the United States, they have been
treated with more consideration, it is owing to the
permeating influence of the Christian religion.

5. They were to be a "by-word," an "astonishment," a "hissing," in the nations where they
were scattered. This again has proved true.

They have been compelled in some cases even to wear a distinctive badge, and occupy what has been invidiously known as the "Jewish quarter."

6. While scattered among all nations, they should still be separate. It is a strange historic phenomenon that this one race is the only one never yet incorporated in, or amalgamated with, the nations among whom they have dwelt. When Irishmen, Scotchmen, Germans and Italians come to America, in the course of a few generations they disappear as such, and become integral parts of one homogeneous American people. But the Jew remains still a Jew; save when by becoming a Christian, he ceases to be distinctively a Jew, and, marrying into Christian families, thus becomes incorporated with Christian Communities.

7. They are to be ultimately restored to their own land, grafted back into their own olive tree, and to have restored to them the Covenant privileges which, during the times of the Gentiles, have been suspended. This remains to be fulfilled.

Any one who is skeptical as to the inspiration of the words of Scripture, should consider whether it is possible that such a complex historic phenomenon as this would or could, without divine foresight, have been clearly foretold by Moses in one of the most ancient books of the human race, and that this prophecy should not only have been fulfilled, but be fulfilling before our eyes at this remote period of time. Surely the foreknowledge of such facts must have been communicated by the omniscient God. It is said that, when one of the great monarchs of Europe asked his chaplain to give him, in one word, an evidence that the Bible was from God, that one word was: "*JEW*."

But, aside from the Jews and the prophecy which centres about them, there is a wider circle of prediction, embracing the whole race, and to which the earliest prophecies of the Holy Scriptures refer. In the ninth chapter of Genesis, 27th verse, it is written—"Cursed be Canaan; a servant of servants shall he be to his brethren. Blessed be Jehovah, God of Shem, and Canaan shall be his servant. God shall enlarge Japheth, and he shall dwell in the tents of Shem, and Canaan shall be his servant."

Here is indicated a threefold distribution of the human race: under Shem, Japheth, and Ham, the father of Canaan. Ham's descendants went to Africa; Japheth's into Europe; Shem's into Asia— three great streams of primeval civilization, beginning after the flood, flowing in different directions, and distributing population among the three continents then known.

The Bible and Prediction

Noah, at this early period, forecast the history and destiny of the Semitic, Japhetic and Hamitic races of the world.

"Blessed be Jehovah, God of Shem." That implies some special relation of Shem to Jehovah, as a Covenant God. The Jews, who are of the race of Shem, became the earliest repositories of the true religion, and from them came, through Jesus Christ, who was of the Semitic stock, the Christian faith.

"God shall enlarge Japheth." No other branch of the human race has known a like enlargement, both as to numerous progeny and as to extensive territory. The Japhetic peoples have been the one enterprising branch of humanity. The Semitic and Hamitic races have never so spread in colonies and by conquests over the face of the earth, as have the Japhetic from Europe into Asia, and America, controlling territory to such a degree that the Japhetic sceptre more than any other sways the world. The sun in his course never sets on his dominions, and surely Japhetic nations, which pride themselves on being foremost in enlargement and conquest, will not question the antiquity or veracity of the prophecy, uttered by Noah.

"He shall dwell in the tents of Shem." The

Semitic races were to be nomadic. Nothing is said about the "tents" of Canaan, or of Japheth. The nomadic races of the human family have principally been Semitic in origin. While they have dwelt in tents, Japheth has not only been enlarged, but has rapidly encroached upon them. By Japheth's dwelling in the tents of Shem may be typically forecast also the fact that the Japhetic races have gone to the Semitic, for their religious faith.

As to Canaan, it is three times averred that he shall be a servant of servants, to his brethren; that is, a slave—the lowest and basest of servants. The fact is indisputable, that the world's slaves have come, in the vast majority of instances, from the descendants of Ham. Terrible, indeed, have been the ravages of the slave trade, carried on round the coast of Africa, for which, during many years, both Great Britain and the United States were responsible, until, after many centuries, God chose, by the voice and pen of Wilberforce and his colleagues in Britain, and afterward by the hammer of Abraham Lincoln in America, to cleave the fetters from millions of bondsmen, and this blot was wiped off from their national escutcheons. So extensive has been African slavery that, if the entire number of natives sacrificed, in capturing victims in the Dark Continent, transporting them through the middle passage, and incorporating them as slaves with other peoples, were reckoned, their bodies would make a double row round the earth at its equator!

When Noah, coming out of the ark to face a new world, became a second father to the race, God drew for him the great lines of civilization, which even to this day are indisputable historical verities.

The second and seventh chapters of Daniel record two visions of the history of the world. The first was given to Nebuchadnezzar, as the first head of what the Bible treats as world-empire, in a dream, which he was unable to recall, but which was in a night-vision communicated to Daniel, also, together with its interpretation. The entire course of future world-empire was outlined—the six hundred years, between Nebuchadnezzar's assumption of the throne and the birth of the Lord Jesus Christ, with hints of a still remoter period. As these predictions are on record, it is easy to test them by the facts of history.

This prophecy is remarkably framed. The first vision is under the figure of a colossal image, no doubt suggesting to Nebuchadnezzar the actual statue erected shortly afterward in the Plain of Dura. The head was of gold; the breast and arms, of silver; the belly and thighs, of brass; the legs, of iron; the feet, of iron and clay, divided into five toes on each foot, suggesting ten smaller kingdoms as the final outcome.

The human head and breast are dual in structure —two eyes, two ears, two parts of the brain, two nostrils—and the upper part of the trunk suggests a more marked duality—two arms, two lungs, two sets of ribs proceeding from the sternum and uniting in the backbone, all this figuratively suggesting a dual empire. The legs suggest not only duality, but division and separation, finally carried to the point of subdivision of two into ten.

This was a singularly accurate forecast of facts of history. Nebuchadnezzar represented a dual empire, the Assyro-Babylonian, Babylon having succeeded to and incorporating the previous Assyrian with its glory. This was the head of gold.

After this was the Medo-Persian kingdom, represented by Cyrus, son-in-law to the Median king, and son of the Persian king. This was the breast and arms of silver.

Alexander, the Macedonian, whose universal conquests made him the next in order of the world's emperors, represented a somewhat closer unity than was found under Nebuchadnezzar or Cyrus. He represented the belly and thighs of brass. The

end of the Macedonian era was the proper beginning of the Roman era, this empire incorporating
into itself what remained of these previous world
kingdoms and their glory. This new epoch is
suggested in the two legs, which may well represent the division of the Roman Empire into the
eastern and western kingdoms, with their centers on
the Tiber and the Bosphorous (395 A.D.), remaining
still, after over two thousand years, distinct, one
from the other. The period when the feet divide
into the ten toes, or the eastern and western kingdoms ramify into ten others, is thought by most
prophetic students to belong to the end of this
dispensation, and immediately to precede that
millennial kingdom of Christ which is to be erected
on the ruins of all others.*

Daniel saw a stone, cut out of the mountain
without hands, smite the image on the feet of
iron and clay, thus reducing the whole image
to powder, which was swept away like the chaff
from summer threshing floors; the stone itself
becoming a great mountain and filling the whole
earth. There seems here a distinction between
"*regnum lapidis*"—the kingdom of the stone—
and "*regnum montis*"—the kingdom of the mountain. The former, we are now under; the latter

*Daniel ii.

probably stands for the reign of Christ in the millennium. The stone is already cut out without hands, but is not yet the mountain filling the whole earth. The smiting of the image is yet future, and the comminution process probably awaits the signal judgments at the end of this dispensation.

The material degeneration of this image, from the gold of the head to the iron and clay of the feet, indicates a gradual degeneracy of the monarchial idea—exactly what history reveals. The strength of monarchy lies in absolutism—undisputed rule; its ideal is unlimited imperial power. Nebuchadnezzar was such an absolute despot; but, in the days of Cyrus, the monarchial idea became mixed up and corrupted with the aristocratic; and in the days of Alexander, the aristocratic further degenerated into favoritism; until, in the days of the Romans, monarchy and aristocracy were leavened with republicanism, and at last developed into oligarchy approaching closely to anarchy. This gradual decline from the monarchial ideal is thus, under the figure of this image, traced from the original absolutism through the successive stages of degeneracy, till the final weakness is indicated in the brittleness of elements which, though combined, cannot be united or assimilated.

In the seventh chapter of Daniel, the same

truths appear, but under different symbols. What Nebuchadnezzar had seen outlined in a majestic image, Daniel saw forecast in a succession of wild beasts coming out of a stormy sea, which in the Scriptures stands for worldly society in commotion and revolution; the beasts, coming up out of it, indicating tyrannical, despotic and cruel tyrants and conquerers, or popular idol chiefs, who develop out of the midst of revolutionary conditions. Daniel saw first a lion with eagle's wings; then a bear—one-sided, with three ribs in its mouth; then a leopard with four wings and four heads; and last, a nondescript beast as strong as iron and using its strength with destructive violence. Why the difference of representation? To Nebuchadnezzar, the monarch of the world, world-empire was naturally revealed as a gigantic figure of worldly majesty; but to Daniel, who by divine insight, could, through this deceptive glamour and glory, perceive the inward carnal corruption, bestial sensuality and cruelty, and God-defying arrogance of these world-empires—they were seen under the form of wild beasts.

Accurate historical truth is again wrapped up in this imagery. The lion with the eagle's wings, still the symbol of Assyria, may be seen in the British Museum, taken out of the palaces of Nineveh

—exactly what Daniel saw as the representatives of the Assyro-Babylonian empire,—the only case in history where the lion has been thus sculptured with eagle's wings,—a lion for majesty of power; an eagle for swiftness of flight.

The bear was one-sided, the Persian element dominating the Median; and the three ribs in the mouth, doubtless represent Babylon, Lydia and Egypt, devoured in cruel wars of aggression.

The leopard, spotted to represent the variety of nationalities grouped under Alexander's conquests, subtle and treacherous, stealthy, rapid and soft-footed in movement; the four wings expressing wide conquests—north, south, east and west— and the four heads, the final division of the empire at Alexander's death among his captains, Cassander, Lysimachus, Ptolemy, and Seleucus.

These beasts were followed by the nondescript animal, representing Rome,—strong as iron, with teeth that break in pieces and bruise, and yet, doomed to grow weaker, and ultimately become a prey to other nations.

These historical facts were thus embodied in the book of Daniel, in a double series of symbols, long before they became real in the annals of the race.

The dream of Nebuchadnezzar and the vision of Daniel leave no room for honest doubt that He whose Omniscient eyes glance over the whole field of the future, and whose Providence shapes history, unveiled to this king and to His own seer the things that were to come to pass thereafter, and of which the students of history have since been, and are now, observers and witnesses.

A brief resumé of the argument may be not unfitting at this point:

The Bible contains in both Testaments nearly one thousand predictions, of which seven hundred or eight hundred, perhaps, belong to the Old, and the rest to the New. Of these predictions, the majority are already accomplished; others being either in process of accomplishment or about to be fulfilled in times approaching.

Applying the criteria as to remoteness of time, these predictions were recorded from four hundred to twenty-four hundred years before the events. As to minuteness of detail, on the basis of compound probability the possibility of a chance coincidence between prediction and event is so incalculably small that even mathematical figures fail to convey any adequate conception of it.

As to novelty of combination, absolutely no precedents have been furnished by previous historic occurrences whereby any man, however sagacious, could have conjectured what was to take place. Such mystery of contradiction is found in the paradoxes these predictions present that even the seers themselves did not understand their own predictions, history alone being capable of interpreting their marvellous and mysterious characters.

The argument from prophecy is designed to supply a natural rational basis for belief in a supernatural Being and a supernatural book. Such a belief is faith's forerunner, preparing its way by convincing the reason; when as yet one cannot see clearly to accept the Bible as the word of God, and Christ as His Son, prediction marks out a path leading surely up to the vestibule where faith enters the temple of truth; he who follows this path comes to a reasonable, intelligent faith, and an equally reasonable, intelligent obedience. The province of reason and the province of faith are thus mutual counterparts.

Reason is first to determine whether the Bible is the Book of God; then what it contains; and then what relation its contents have to the reader. When reason has explored, and satisfied itself on these three matters, then the way is clear for faith to accept the Bible as the Word of God, and its contents in their relation to faith and life. If inscrutable mysteries are afterward found in the

The Bible and Prediction

Bible which reason cannot comprehend or explain, the believer properly falls back upon the fact that he has found the book evidenced as the Word of God; and, as there must be in God's mind much that man's little mind cannot follow, it is no blind credulity but an intelligent and reasonable faith that still impels to self surrender.

When it becomes necessary to have a serious operation performed upon the vital organs in order to save from death, what does a reasonable man do? First of all, he finds out, on rational grounds, whether a surgeon of whom he has heard is competent to take his disease in hand, and deal with it skilfully. Then he satisfies himself that such surgeon is not a man of malice, and will take no opportunity, because of his patient's helplessness, to inflict any injury or unnecessary suffering. When a man has thus satisfied himself that the surgeon is skilful, experienced, competent and benevolent, he gives up himself to his care, lies on his operating table, inhales the anæsthetic, and leaves himself passive in his hands.

Somewhat so God says to us: "Here is the evidence that I am God; that I have spoken; that the contents of this Book are My own utterances; are addressed to you, and have a vital relation to your spiritual well being in this world and in the

world to come." So now, having approached the
vestibule of faith by this pathway of intelligent
reason, one is prepared to submit himself to God,
allow Him with full consent to take charge of him,
and even to insert the knife that cuts away the
cancer or the tumour, while he lies helpless in the
great Physician's hands. He can trust Him to do
what He will; and, if His processes transcend alike
his own experience and intelligence, he remembers
how he has previously satisfied himself that He
is infinitely skilful, competent and benevolent;
that in Him infinite wisdom makes mistakes of
judgment impossible, and infinite love makes
mistakes of malice equally impossible. His book
may contain much that cannot be interpreted by
present experience and finite intelligence, so that
we cannot always tell what reasons lie behind
His commands, or what possibilities lie in the
scope of His promises; yet when we give up ourselves to Him, such implicit trust is not the fruit of
credulity, but the triumph of reason, the natural
outcome of an assurance created by intelligent
inquiry. Such a believer is not the victim of a
blind unreasoning confidence, but the victor over
carnal unbelief, and the lies and wiles of the great
adversary who is the maligner of God and the
betrayer of man!

CHAPTER VI

THE BIBLE AND CHRIST

THE heart of our theme and the inmost core of the Bible testimony is *The Person of the Son of God.*

However costly the casket which contains a pearl of great price, its value lies mainly in the gem that it holds. The greatest question of all as to the Oracles of God, is what witness do they bear to the Messiah? The question whether Jesus Christ is the Son of God, and the Saviour of men— this the Bible answers with supreme care and absolute certainty.

The whole Old Testament is pervaded by prophecies of Christ. Leaving the indirect predictions for subsequent consideration, we now consider the direct forecasts concerning Him; and, because it is impracticable to examine the whole of this body of prophecy within such narrow limits, it may be well to select, almost at random, some leading passages from different parts of the Old Testament on which especially to concentrate attention.

(1.) First of all, Genesis III:15. Immediately

after the fall of man, occurs this primal prophecy of the seed of the woman—the promise of a Redeemer. This is also the germ of all messianic prophecy that follows, down to the close of Malachi; hence it is well to look closely at this germinal prediction and conception.

God said to the Serpent: "And I, Jehovah, will put enmity between thee and the woman,

"And between thy seed and her seed:

"It shall bruise (or crush) thy head,

"And thou shalt bruise (or crush) his heel."

This is a magnificent pictorial metaphor. It suggests a human form, with his heel upon the head of a serpent, crushing the life out of the head— his higher part—while the serpent is planting his venomous fangs in his victor's heel—his lower part.

This shows how much a very short prediction may contain and suggest. It presents, in outline, the new representative seed, the Second Man, the Last Adam. He is the Seed of the *woman*—nothing is said about his being the offspring of the *man* —a significant omission, and the words of Jehovah which follow are addressed, first of all, to the woman, the coming Deliverer being specifically and emphatically called *her* "seed." There is to be eternal enmity between the principle represented by the serpent—the Devil—and that represented by the Seed of the woman. Again the Seed of the woman is to deal a death blow on the serpent, but the latter is to be permitted at the same time to inflict a sting upon the heel that crushes him. Last of all, this is all due to a divine arrangement: "*I will put enmity* between thee and the woman."

As the oak is germinally in the acorn, and the eagle in the egg, all subsequent Messianic prophecies of the Old Testament are here in germ. There is scarcely added, in the whole aftercourse of such prophecy, one idea that is absolutely new, other predictions growing out of and expanding this germinal prediction.

Christ is further on revealed as a priest, but here His priesthood is foreshadowed in His wounding by Satan—He is a Vicarious Sufferer. Christ is to be a king; here the suggestion of His kingship is found in His victory over the Devil and his works. Thus, as the Messianic idea is followed out through the Old Testament, this germ is seen to expand and ramify, thus containing in substance all the others.

(2.) Moses gives to the Children of Israel a prediction of a great prophet that is to arise:

"The Lord thy God shall raise up unto thee a prophet,

"From the midst of thee,

"Of thy brethren, like unto me.

"Unto Him shall ye hearken."

"I, Jehovah, will put My words in his mouth.

"Whosoever will not hearken unto My words

"Which He shall speak in my name,

"I will require it of him."*

A great prophet was to be specially raised up by God to come out of the tribes of Israel, and to have a certain likeness to Moses; but to be invested with unique authority as the mouthpiece of God; and to reject His authoritative utterances will bring the hearer into judgment. Thus, in one verse of twenty-eight words, we have a suggestive prediction of the coming Prophet, as in Genesis III., of the coming Priest and King.

(3.) The twenty-second Psalm. This is specifically the Crucifixion Psalm, the one fragment of Old Testament scripture that plainly presents Christ *on the cross*. Here is a suffering victim; His hands and feet, pierced; stripped of His raiment, and partially nude so that others can look on His bones; they that pass by mock and deride Him, shooting out the lip; His mortal agony is attended with extreme thirst. The Psalm opens with the Atonement cry: "My God, My God, why hast Thou forsaken me!" and

* Deuteronomy XVIII: 15–19.

106

another of his cries on the cross may be heard in
the last verse: "Shall declare His righteousness
unto a people that shall be born:" "IT IS
FINISHED!"* In fact, the seven sentences on the
Cross may be found, at least *suggested*, in the course
of this poem.

More than this, it is a *"Psalm of Sobs."*† The
Hebrew shows not one *completed sentence* in the
opening verses; but a series of brief ejaculations,
like the gasps of a dying man whose breath and
strength are failing, and who can only utter a word
or two at a time: "My God—My God—Why forsaken me—far from helping me!—words of My
roaring!—" There is something overwhelmingly
pathetic in this Psalm, when the reader sees in it
his suffering Saviour, gasping for life, unable to
articulate one continuous sentence. From these
lines tears seem to drip and blood seems to drop.
The writer thus forecasts that mystery of the cross,
which remained unsolved for a thousand years. It
was like a dark cavern at the time; but when the
gospel narrative portrays Jesus as the crucified
one, it is like putting a lighted torch in the cavern,
revealing radiant crystals.

(4.) The ninth chapter of Isaiah, sixth verse,

* Original Hebrew,
† Bishop Alexander, "Witness of The Psalms to Christ"

not known to be a prophecy of Messiah until it was, as such, quoted in the New Testament.

"For unto us a child is born;

"Unto us a son is given:

"And the government shall be upon His shoulder;

"And His name shall be called Wonderful, Counsellor,

"The Mighty God, The Everlasting Father,

"The Prince of Peace."

"Unto us a child is born" suggests the human nature of Christ; "Unto us a Son is given," that suggests the divine side; "And the government shall be upon His shoulder." here is kingship; "And His name shall be called Wonderful:" Matthew shows the correspondence between Him and the prophecies concerning Him; "Counsellor:" Luke introduces Him as Man's Friend and Counsellor. "The Mighty God:" in Mark He is seen as the Mighty Worker; "The Everlasting Father:" John shows Him identical with the Father, from Everlasting; "The Prince of Peace:" In the Acts of the Apostles the Prince of Life is seen, beginning His career of conquest, with spiritual and not carnal weapons.

Here, then, are forecasts of His humanity, divinity and kingship; and his fivefold character as in the Gospel narratives and the Acts of the Apostles.

Prophecies of Christ

(5.) The fifty-third chapter of Isaiah. Twenty-seven continuous chapters, from the fortieth to the sixty-sixth, constitute one great Messianic poem of the Old Testament. The only divisions in the original are those marked by the refrain: "There is no peace, saith my God, to the wicked." which recurs at the end of the first and the second third, dividing the poem into three about equal parts. In the center of the middle part, and so of the whole poem, is this fifty-third chapter—the one unquestionable prophecy of Jesus Christ as the Lamb of God, vicariously suffering for man.*

Marvellous chapter, indeed! containing only twelve verses, yet fourteen times announcing the doctrine of vicarious sacrifice for sin: "He hath borne our griefs.—Carried our sorrows.—Was wounded for our transgressions.—Was bruised for our iniquities.—The chastisement of our peace was upon Him.—With His stripes we are healed.—The Lord hath laid upon Him the iniquity of us all.—Thou shalt make His soul an offering for sin.—By His knowledge shall My righteous servant justify many.—He shall bear their iniquities.

The whole chapter overflows with this conception and never was its mystery solved until the Lord Jesus Christ was made sin for us. Those who

*Acts, VIII: 28–36.

question its reference to Jesus Christ, forget that the Holy Spirit, through Philip, taught the Etheopian eunuch that He is here meant, so that we have Him who inspired, also to interpret.

This chapter is also an example of the mystery of contradiction, for it is a bundle of paradoxes or apparent contradictions, as numerous as the verses of the chapter. "He is a root out of the dry ground, yet fruitful; He has no form nor beauty, yet is the chosen servant of God; He is despised of men, yet the appointed Saviour; He suffers unto death, yet He survives; He has no offspring, yet has a numerous seed; He makes His grave with the wicked, yet is buried in the sepulchre of the rich; He suffers adversity, yet enjoys prosperity; He is triumphed over, yet He triumphs; He is despoiled, yet He despoils; He is cut off in the midst of His days, and yet prolongs His days; He is condemned Himself, yet He justifies the condemned. These paradoxes remained a problem until the cross was set up, and the sepulchre burst open, and the Son of God, Who came down to die, went up to reign. The suffering Messiah and the reigning Saviour are here seen as one, but the mystery of this union could by subsequent history only be made plain.

(6.) Daniel, ninth chapter, twenty-fourth

verse: "Seventy weeks are determined upon thy people.

"Know therefore, and understand, that from the going forth of the commandment to restore and build Jerusalem, unto the Messiah, the Prince, shall be seven weeks, and three score and two weeks." The Hebrew word is "heptades" or periods of seven. Seventy times seven years is four hundred and ninety. There are three or four ways by which the sacred number of years have been reckoned. One decree to restore and rebuild Jerusalem, went forth four hundred and fifty-seven years before Christ; if the thirty-three years of Christ's earthly sojourn be added, it gives exactly four hundred and ninety—four hundred and fifty-seven plus thirty-three.

*Sir Robert Anderson gives perhaps the most satisfactory calculation yet made, showing that it was exactly to a day the four hundred and eighty-three years prophesied in the ninth chapter of Daniel, from the time of the going forth of the commandment until Jesus entered into Jerusalem in the capacity of the Messianic Prince, riding upon an ass, and a colt the foal of an ass.

(7.) Micah, fifth chapter, second verse:

"But thou, Bethlehem Ephratah, though thou

*"Daniel in the Critics' Den."

be little among the thousands of Judah, yet out of thee shall He come forth unto me that is to be ruler in Israel; whose goings forth have been from of old, from everlasting."

Here is the prophecy of a governor to come out of Bethlehem. That village is to be the place of His birth, who is to be Ruler in Israel; yet He is one whose goings forth have been not only from antiquity, but from eternity.

There is no question about whom that prophecy forecasts. But Christ's virgin mother did not live at Bethlehem, but at Nazareth; and it was not very likely that, on the eve of the primal sorrow of her sex, she would needlessly travel over hot and dusty roads from one village to the other. But the decree that the Roman world should be taxed, compelled all who were subject to taxation to go to the place from which the family hailed, and be enrolled; and so, although that tax was not collected till eight years later, God thus brought that virgin mother from Nazareth to Bethlehem at the precise time which would fulfill the prediction of Micah.*

* Those "wise men from the East," came probably from Persia, the land of Daniel; and, if they had Daniel's prophecy, they knew that the *time* for the Messiah's birth had about come, but if they had not also Micah's prophecy, which foretells it to be at Bethlehem, they might not have known *where* he was to be born, and so they followed the star to Jerusalem to inquire of the scribes there as to the *place*.

Prophecies of Christ

Our selection has been limited to seven passages only from the Old Testament concerning Messiah: Gen. III, Deut. XVIII, Psalm XXII, Daniel IX, Micah V, Isaiah IX, and Isaiah LIII; and yet here is one consistent progressive unfolding of Messianic prophecy. The first contains the germ of the rest, outlining the general scheme of deliverance, through the woman's seed.

Deuteronomy forecasts His prophetic office.

Psalm XXII, the Psalm of the Crucifixion, the priestly.

Isaiah IX, His double nature, as Child of Man and Son of God,—the kingly.

Isaiah LIII, His vicarious suffering for sin.

Micah gives the place of His birth; and

Daniel, the time of His birth.

Again we may apply the criteria of prophecy, heretofore laid down as tests:

(1.) Remoteness of Time. Between the Old and New Testaments is a gap of four hundred years, during which no prophecies are recorded, which so divides the two periods as to make impossible any collusion between the Old Testament prophets and New Testament evangelists. Men cannot reach hands across the gap of four centuries, whether for good or evil purposes, either for combination or conspiracy; and this interval of silence makes sure that those who wrote the prophecies could have had no part in bringing the predictions to pass.

(2.) Minutiæ of Detail. Over three hundred predictions about the Messiah are found in the Old Testament. According to the law of compound probability, the chance of their coming true is represented by a fraction whose numerator is one, and the denominator eighty-four, followed by nearly one hundred ciphers! One might almost as well expect by accident to happen to dip up any one particular drop out of the ocean as to expect so many prophetic rays to converge by chance upon one man, in one place, at one time. God has put especially upon these prophecies as to His Son, the stamp of absolute verity and indisputable certainty, that we may know whom we have believed. Mistakes in so solemn a matter are fatal and God meant that none should be possible.

(3.) Novelty of Combination. Nothing was ever like this before. Never a human child who was also a Divine Son—at the same time wounded by the Devil and crushing him—never another who was appointed Saviour, yet crucified as a malefactor—Who died, and yet lived—could not save Himself, and yet saved others. Such paradoxes are not only without precedent, but defy explanation unless they refer to Jesus Christ.

To sum up the argument, the prophetic Scriptures fully vindicate the honour and majesty and deity of the Lord and Saviour Jesus Christ. This is a vital issue with every believer, since his salvation hangs on the truth of these prophecies, and the reality of the claims of the Son of God, and to one who devoutly searches for evidence, ample proof is at hand.

The accuracy of prediction is most minute. As Christ was to be born, He must be born of some of the families of the earth. Every time a new marriage issues in offspring, from some of these new branches of the family tree, one must be selected from which God's Messianic Flower is to spring and bloom. One mistake would be fatal. From Noah's three sons, Shem, Ham and Japheth, Shem is chosen; from Abraham's two sons, Isaac and Ishmael, Isaac; from Isaac's two sons, Jacob and Esau, Jacob; Jacob's family tree has twelve new branches and Judah is the fruitful branch. Every time prophecy makes a particular choice, there is new risk, humanly speaking, of selecting the wrong branch, and so of falsifying facts, and nothing short of absolute accuracy will do when God claims to speak.

Again Messiah must have a birthplace. Three continents—Europe, Asia and Africa—were known to the ancient world; Asia is chosen. But Asia has many countries—one of them is indicated, a little country known as the Land of Promise—Palestine or Syria. Here were three districts: Judea, Galilee and Samaria; it is Judea that is the elect one. But here again are many villages; out of these "thousands" the favoured one is little Bethlehem. But as Bethlehem means "House of Bread," the name might stand for more than one village located in a fertile tract; and so, to make prediction more definite and certain, it is "Bethlehem, in the land of *Judah*." The prophet puts his finger on one obscure village on the map of the world; but he speaks infallibly, for the Omniscient God was behind his utterance.

Messiah must be born at some *time*. It might have been in any century and any year, but with absolute certainty the exact year is foretold.

Old Testament prophecy is God's "Plant of Renown." It grows from its primitive germ, and branches into minute twigs and remains a mystery for many centuries. Just what it means and what it is there for, man knows not clearly. Now and then one of the old-time believers or godly men, like David, sees Christ dimly foreshadowed in these predictions; but when history comes and touches twig after twig, they burst into bloom; and now the Plant of Renown becomes a burning bush, and the place is holy ground. Inspired argument! Absolute certainty! Divine verity! There would be no honest infidel in the world were Messianic prophecy studied, nor any doubting disciple if this body of prediction were understood. Here is God's Rock of Ages, whether or not we know how unshakable is faith's standing place, and how needless it is to be discouraged when attacks are made on the Word of God.

Sometimes history seems to have been moved backward, and the tragedy of the suffering of Christ is re-enacted. Men are again striking Him with the rod, spitting in His face, passing Him by and deriding Him. And alas! He is being also wounded even in the "house of His friends," and crucified afresh before a dying world. Well may we therefore rejoice to vindicate His assaulted majesty and dignity by appealing to those Old Testament prophecies concerning Him, which are to a candid mind so conclusive and convincing.

One seldom meets an unconverted inquirer who seems absolutely without prejudice on religious subjects. Once a young Japanese came to the writer of these pages. He had been sent over by

his government to study questions of Western
civilization, philosophy and science. He had
found that his Buddhism would not stand investigation, and, satisfied that it was a false faith, had
cast away his idolatry and superstitions—a man
absolutely without any religion. Infidels there
are a plenty, but they are not without a religion of
their own, for infidelity is the worst kind of a false
faith, with the worst sort of a creed. They who
affirm that they believe nothing, believe the most
incredible things. But this man was no infidel.
He had cast away his idols to the moles and bats
and abandoned his ancestral traditions, but his
mind was like a sheet of blank paper on which truth
might be written, and his frank words revealed his
condition: "I have heard something of Christianity and I want to know whether it is the true
religion." With Bible in hand we together went
over the body of Messianic prophecy. A little
book prepared for doubting minds—"Many Infallible Proofs"—was put into his hands and he went
away, but came back shortly after a firm believer
in Jesus Christ, and afterward returned to Japan to
teach his countrymen how the prophecies of the
Old Testament found their accomplishment in the
Christ of the New; and that without doubt the
Book is inspired, and Christ is the Son of God. The

path by which he arrived at that rational faith was the study of Messianic prediction.

It is of vast importance to get before every man and woman the scope of this argument—this most neglected department of study—the prophecies of the Old Testament with regard to the Lord Jesus Christ.

A double argument is found in them: first they absolutely authenticate the Old Testament as an inspired book; and, second, they absolutely authenticate Jesus Christ as the Son of God. It is alike inconceivable that such a body of prophecy could have been mere guess-work or have found its place in any merely human production; and that so many predictions should point forward to one individual in the future, who is either a knave or an impostor, a deluded fanatic or an insane fool. The prophecies move as in procession before the Person of Christ and, like soldiers, salute Him as their general-in-chief, and He, to whom they thus pay homage, must be none other than He "Whose goings forth have been from of old, even from everlasting."

These are only, however, direct predictions, and but a few even of them; but they suffice to banish all reasonable doubt when we consider the remoteness of the time in which they were spoken; and

the surprising minuteness of detail to which they
descend, even to His birth of a virgin mother, the
number of pieces of silver given for His betrayal,
His silence before His accusers, and His meek and
unresisting submission before His crucifiers, the
dying sentences on the cross, the hooting, mocking,
insulting language of those that passed by, the
piercing of hands and feet, His agonizing thirst,
the double disposition of His raiment.*   In view
of these and hundreds of other particulars, successively unfolded during the long period covered
by Old Testament writings, it is absolutely inconceivable that all this could have been a mere chance
coincidence of forecast and fulfilment.

She was an extraordinary Queen who lately sat
on the throne of the British Empire, and for a
longer time than any other monarch of history.
At the time of her coronation, there was a series
of magnificent festivities in honour of her accession
to the throne, and, last of them all, the performance of that great oratorio of "The Messiah,"
which is such a favourite with British audiences.
The Queen presided, and she had been told by those

* Here is another paradox, "They parted my garments among them,
and upon my vesture did they cast lots." Psa. xxii : 1, 8. If they
parted His garments, why did they need to cast lots?   They distributed
the lesser attire, but as to His circular, seamless robe, they said : "It is
a pity to rend it; let us cast lots whose it shall be."   So the double
prophecy was literally fulfilled.

who were familiar with court manners that, though it is customary with the British public to arise, when the opening notes are struck of "The Hallelujah Chorus," and to remain standing until it is finished, it would be a violation of her Imperial dignity if she should rise with the multitude, as it is the royal prerogative to sit when others stand. When the chorus began, and the great multitude rose to their feet, she yearned to stand up and so confess with them her allegiance to the Messiah in whose honour the chorus was sung; but she remembered her instructions, and the modest young woman, who was scarcely yet familiar with royal dignity, kept her seat as the words rang out, "Hallelujah, Hallelujah, For the Lord God Omnipotent reigneth." But, when in the last part of the chorus, the words pealed out—"King of Kings, and Lord of Lords," she forgot her court instructions and her royal dignity, and, rising to her feet and folding her arms across her breast, she bowed her head with the crown of empire upon it.

To a devout believer, the whole Bible is one Oratorio of the Messiah. Prediction joins prediction in one Hallelujah Chorus—"Hallelujah, Hallelujah! For the Lord God Omnipotent reigneth." And, as the climax is reached, and the promised Seed of the woman and the crucified

Christ is seen to be the King of Kings and Lord
of Lords, he cannot maintain an attitude of indifference.   He must join the great cloud of witness-
bearers and cannot keep silence, and he sings:

> "Bring forth the royal diadem,
> And crown Him Lord of All."

Amen

CHAPTER VII

THE BIBLE AND INDIRECT FORECAST

The waters of the Pool of Siloam, outside of the city of Jerusalem, have their fountains underneath the ancient site of the temple on Moriah. Those springs discharged their waters through a subterranean passage and came up in Siloam's Pool—then, again following an underground conduit, appeared in another pool farther on; and then, following still another subterranean passage to the Gardens of Solomon, distributed their irrigating and fertilizing influences and promoted fertility. Dr. Edward Robinson, of New York, crawled on his hands and knees through this subterranean passage, in order positively to ascertain whether such hidden channels existed.

The Messianic Conception, springing from beneath the Throne of God, follows hidden channels, coming up now and then in clear, direct messianic prediction; then, following other courses beneath the surface, opens up in Messianic history, and so waters and fertilizes the whole Garden of the Lord; and when the student, in a devout frame of mind, studies, under the control of the Spirit, the prophecy and the history, and traces even those concealed and indirect suggestions of the coming of Christ, he finds everywhere new unfoldings of the Messianic idea.

These *Indirect Prophecies* about the Lord Jesus Christ now claim attention. Two passages of Scripture at the outset need careful comparison.

In Luke xxiv, we have a record of an informal discourse of our Lord, while going with two disciples from Jerusalem to Emmaus. On that occasion of His post-resurrection appearance and converse—"beginning at Moses and all the prophets, He expounded unto them in all the Scriptures the things concerning Himself" (verse 24). Still more definitely He said: "All things must be fulfilled which are written in the law of Moses and in the prophets and in the Psalms concerning Me" (verse 44).

The Old Testament scriptures were popularly divided into these three main parts: (1) The Law, or the historical books; (2) The Psalms, or the poetical; (3) and the Prophets, or the prophetical. This division, though not exact, was the current way of classification, and is still followed in the Hebrew Old Testament. Christ, therefore, showed His disciples how they could

start with Moses—the beginning—follow the
course of the Law or historical writings, pass
into the Psalms, the poetical and devotional,
and then through the whole group of prophetical
books, and in all those scriptures trace things concerning Himself which must needs be fulfilled.

Where our Lord has spoken, it is ours to be
silent, hear and learn. If any one doubts or
denies that there are such intimations in the Old
Testament scripture, it is enough to refer him to the
authority of the Master. It must take nothing
short of audacity to venture any such denial in
face of this post-resurrection assurance from the
Lord Himself.

How did this discourse come to be known to
Luke? The Lord promised that the Holy Spirit
should bring to their remembrance the things that
He had said to them; and ordinarily it is safe to
infer that, where anything is recorded, the party
recording it was present on the occasion; and there
is little reason to doubt that it was Luke himself
who was with Cleopas, and was the other unnamed
disciple who, on this journey from Jerusalem to
Emmaus, heard these marvellous words of Christ.

In the Epistle to the Hebrews, there is what
seems to be the substance of this discourse of our
Lord to these two disciples. All readers of the

Word have felt how gladly they would have been with those three, that day, and had their hearts burn within them "while He opened to them the Scriptures;" and the question has often been raised whether there is any hint in the Bible of what Christ said on that occasion. Possibly we may find such a hint in this Epistle to the Hebrews. Luke was the companion of Paul, and it is generally conceded that, if Paul did not write this anonymous letter to the Hebrews, he, who did, wrote at Paul's dictation or with his coöperation and under his immediate guidance. If this be true, how likely it would be that Luke should have communicated to Paul, his companion, the substance of this conversation; and so in the Epistle to the Hebrews the substance of that discourse is reproduced. This seems the more likely, as this is the only letter in the New Testament which shows, on a large scale, how the Old Testament Scriptures contain indirect as well as direct predictions of the Lord Jesus Christ.

For instance, the contents of the first ten chapters present before us six or seven ways in which the Old Testament foreshadows Christ: (1) Typical characters and offices; (2) typical structure and furniture in the tabernacle; (3) typical rites and ceremonies; (4) typical events and scenes; (5) typical fasts and feasts; (6) typical sayings and doings; (7) typical precepts and prohibitions. All these are drawn from the Old Testament, and used by the writer of this Epistle to prove that, even where no direct prediction is found, indirect forecasts referring to Christ may be distinctly traced. In these ten chapters it is curious that seven words are used, indicating the typical character of Old Testament teaching. For instance, the word *"order:"* "After the order (or rank) of Melchisedec;" *"Likeness"* or *"similitude,"* used of the same party; *"shadow;"* *"example;"* *"parable;" "type;" "anti-type;"** these words or their equivalents occur in the chapters referred to; we give the English equivalents of the original terms; for instance, the word *"parable"* does not occur in the English version, but in the ninth chapter, eighth verse, in the Greek. Not only have we these seven words, to indicate that we may find typical teaching in the Old Testament, but it is distinctly said in the ninth chapter, eighth verse,— ("The Holy Ghost *this signifying"*)—that the Holy Spirit, in these types of the Old Testament, signified or forecast Messianic truth. It is certainly noteworthy that the intimation is twice given by Luke, that Christ unfolded the things

* παραβολη, ωποξειγμα, σκια, ταξις, ομοιοτης, τυπος αντιτυπος.

concerning Himself in the law of Moses, the Psalms, and the Prophets; and then, in the Epistle to the Hebrews, it would seem as though the very substance of that discourse is unfolded by divine illumination to the mind of the writer, so that we can trace in a large part of the Old Testament, these typical characters and offices, events and sayings, rites and ceremonies.

What pertains specially to the atoning work of the Lord Jesus Christ, constitutes, in itself, a body of testimony deserving special notice; but at present we notice some of the forecasts, found in these ancient types and parables, or, as they are called in one place, allegories—* that is, without denying their historical value as facts, hinting that, beneath the historical facts, lies another and deeper meaning, to be unfolded.

For instance, the epistle refers to certain typical characters and offices. In the first few chapters we have four such typical personages: (1) Adam, (2) Moses, (3) Aaron, (4) Melchisedec. Adam forecasts Christ as the Second Man, the Last Adam. Adam was created a prophet, by immediate intuition to know the will of God; a priest, having the right to stand before God in specially intimate relationship; and a king, having the sceptre of

*Galatians v:24 αλληγορουμενα.

dominion over the visible creation; so that he embodied in himself these three parallel functions. When he fell, he ceased to be a prophet, and needed a teacher; he ceased to be a priest, and needed a mediator; he ceased to be a king, and needed a sovereign to reign over him and regain for him his lost sceptre. All this the Seed of the woman was to accomplish. He was to be God's Prophet to men, to teach God's will; the High Priest, to represent man before God; and the King, to rule man and eventually bring all things in subjection under His feet. This three-fold character of Christ as the Last Adam is further anticipated and forecast in the three great characters of the Old Testament that follow—Moses, Aaron and Melchisedec.

In the third chapter we read: "Consider the *Apostle and High Priest* of our profession:" Apostle —Moses; High Priest—Aaron. An apostle is one sent from God to man, an authorized prophet and teacher; a High Priest is one sent forth from man to God, an appointed representative. Christ as God's apostle comes forth from God to represent Him to man, and as High Priest goes back to God to represent man to God; and so in Moses, the apostle and prophet, and in Aaron, the priest we have two typical characters, representing two aspects of that three-fold character foreshadowed in Adam, and to be fulfilled in the Seed of the woman.

In Melchisedec, a priest-king, this three-fold profile is completely filled out. Moses and Aaron together (brothers jointly sharing the administration) represent Him as the Prophet-Priest; then Melchisedec is presented as the Priest-King, and together the three foreshadow all three great offices of Jesus Christ, and hint, by their combination, that those offices are to be combined in Him.

Typical structure and furniture are shown in the tabernacle, the description of which, with its contents and ritual, occupies more room in the Bible than any other single object or subject in the Old or New Testaments, and there must be a reason for it. Every detail of the tabernacle is described, and seven times in all is reference made to the pattern shown in the Mount,* to emphasize the fact that in no respect, however minute, was that pattern to be disregarded. What was that pattern? The simple diagram opposite may assist to fix on the mind, through the eye, the structure of the Tabernacle. At the rear was the Holiest of all, a perfect cube, ten cubits long, deep and high; in front of it, separated by a

Exod. xxv: 9, 40, xxvi: 30, xxviii: 8. Numbers viii: 4. Acts vii: 44.
Heb. viii: 5. Comp. I. Chron. xxviii: 11, 12, 18, 19.

DIAGRAM of the TABERNACLE AND ITS FURNITURE

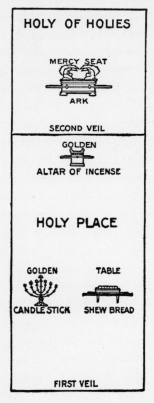

HOLY OF HOLIES

MERCY SEAT

ARK

SECOND VEIL

GOLDEN

ALTAR OF INCENSE

HOLY PLACE

GOLDEN   TABLE

CANDLE STICK   SHEW BREAD

FIRST VEIL

LAVER

OUTER COURT

BRAZEN

ALTAR

veil, the Holy Place, twenty cubits long and ten cubits broad; and, outside another veil, the court.

As to the furniture of the tabernacle: first, outside the first veil and directly in front, as one approached, was the brazen altar of sacrifice, and back of it, the laver. Then, inside of the first veil, the table of shew bread on the right; and on the left, the golden candlestick; then, nearer to the second veil, the golden altar of incense. Beyond this second veil was the Ark, with the mysterious cover—the Mercy Seat, with the Cherubim facing each other, and bowing over it; and, in between them, burned the sacred Shekinah fire.

Here, then, are seven objects that fixed the gaze:

(1.) The Brazen Altar of Sacrifice that stood for atonement by blood.

(2.) The Laver that stood for Regeneration through the Word and through the Spirit, as is plainly taught in the New Testament.

(3.) The Table of Shew Bread, with its oblations and libations,* representing food and drink for the sustentation of life.

(4.) The Golden Candlestick, with its seven branches, type of Christ as the light of the world.

---

* The latter are often overlooked; there seems no question that the cups or bowls on that table represented liquid food, as the " Loaves of Presence " represented solid food.

(5.) The Altar of Incense which stands for prayer and supplication.

(6.) The Mercy Seat, that stands for Intercession, Reconciliation and Identification with God.

(7.) And then the Shekinah Fire, that symbol of the Life of God, and specifically, the Holy Spirit.

That succession of objects, seen by the High Priest as he went into God's presence, represents the entire work of the Lord Jesus Christ from the beginning to the end of His sacrificial and glorious mediation on behalf of man. In the Gospel according to John, the order of truth as there unfolded with regard to the person and work of Jesus Christ, *is exactly correspondent with the order* of these objects in the Tabernacle, and in not one particular is that order violated. In the first chapter—"Behold the Lamb of God, that taketh away the sin of the world"—reminds us of the sacrifices on the Brazen Altar; in the third chapter: "Except a man be born of water and of the Spirit, he cannot enter into the kingdom of God," suggests the Laver of Regeneration; in the fourth and sixth chapters, He is represented as the Drink that satisfies all thirst, and as "the Bread of Life; he that cometh unto Me shall never hunger." Thus, in these chapters, the Table of Shew Bread, with its oblations and libations, is suggested.

Indirect Forecasts

In the eighth and ninth chapters Christ twice distinctly declares "I am the light of the world." Here we are reminded of the golden candlestick, and that suggestion of light runs through; for example, the blind man in the ninth chapter relieved from his blindness from birth, and made to see, is the symbol of the sinner, when the light of the world shines on his darkness and drives it away.

Then, in the fourteenth, fifteenth and sixteenth chapters, we have that seven-fold lesson on "asking in Jesus' name," never before taught—which corresponds to the golden altar of incense; and, in the seventeenth chapter, the great glimpse of His own intercession, and the first and only instance of that general work of intercession,* forecast in the fourteenth chapter, sixteenth verse, "I will pray the Father, and He shall give you another Comforter."

Exactly the order of the sacred furniture of the tabernacle reappears apparently in the truth unfolded here, so that the Apostle John's Gospel narrative becomes, as it were, a new tabernacle of testimony, where we begin at the outer court, go into the holy place, pass the veil into the Holy of

* Compare Luke XXII: 32. This was not general but individual. "I have prayed for *thee*."

Holies, and hear His intercession as He stands before the throne, although not Himself yet permanently withdrawn within that veil.

This veil itself is typical, as we are taught in the Epistle to the Hebrews. It represents "His flesh," which flesh was rent, in order that the salvation of the world might be accomplished, and the believer himself draw near to the Mercy Seat. Here, in this Intercessory Prayer, we have a glimpse of Christ's perpetual mediation beyond the veil. Then, when, having passed through the experience of death, He comes forth from the grave in resurrection power, He ascends on high to send the Holy Spirit to teach the Church the two great and glorious privileges, of which He has thus given the forecast: Access in Him to the Mercy Seat; identification between God and man in Christ:—"My Father, and your Father; My God, and your God." And then the impartation of the Shekinah Fire and Light to us: "Receive ye the Holy Ghost."

Let this startling correspondence not be too hastily passed by.

The tabernacle, constructed in the time of Moses, all the details of which and its furniture are described with minuteness, was not in one particular, to be deviated from in the slightest respect. Connected with this structure were the Brazen

Altar, Laver, Table of Shew Bread, Golden Candle-stick, Altar of Incense, Ark and Mercy Seat with Shekinah Fire,—and, when John writes the last of the gospel narratives—particularly setting forth the Deity of the Son of God, and the fact that by believing in His name we have eternal life—he begins at the Brazen Altar: "Behold the Lamb of God;" he passes to the Laver: "Except a man be born of water and of the Spirit;" he takes us to the Shew Bread Table: "I am the Bread of Life;" he points us to the Golden Candlestick: "I am the Light of the World;" he leads us to the Altar of Incense: "Ask in My name;" and he then gives us a glimpse of things beyond the veil: "My Father, and your Father, My God, and your God;" "And He breathed on them and said, Receive ye the Holy Ghost." Then, by the Holy Spirit's Descent and Indwelling, the believer becomes himself the holiest of all, as taught in the two Epistles to the Corin-thians, where the particular word translated "tem-ple" in the original, means not generally the temple with all its courts, but specifically its inmost shrine.*

Is all this an accident, or is it divine design? and when Jesus Christ, on the way to Emmaus, un-folded in all the Scriptures the great things, there

* Compare ιερον and ναος.

taught concerning Himself, did He not give then the substance of what is recorded in these chapters of the Epistle to the Hebrews with regard to the structure of the tabernacle and its sacred furniture, the priesthood and its offices, as all pointing forward to Him, the Lamb of God, the Light of the World, the Bread of Life, the Great Intercessor, the Mercy Seat, the Giver of the Holy Ghost?

This is but one illustration of the Messianic typology of the Old Testament, but it opens a door to unlimited discovery of truth in the whole recorded history of the Hebrew people. In closing this chapter, a few grand conclusions from this whole argument may be indicated.

First, the Bible is the mirror of the blessed Lord Jesus Christ, or, rather, a series or group of mirrors, in the midst of which He stands, so that some separate aspect of His glorious personality is reflected in each of them in turn. Here is the mirror of direct prediction; there is the mirror of symbol, rite and ceremony; again, the mirror of individual characters and holy offices; the mirror of Levitica precepts and prohibitions; and, again, of sayings and doings which have an allegorical meaning. So all around the great gallery of the Scriptures, these manifold mirrors reflect one consummate and transcendent personality,—the Son of Man and the Son of God.

Not only so, but the whole Bible is again seen to be a prophetic book: there is no point where the line can be drawn so that we can say, "Here prediction begins, and there it ends." Rightly understood, the Bible throughout contains the prophecies and revelations of Jesus.

How different the bird's wings, and the wings which a man makes with which to fly. There have been almost countless experiments in the way of attempts to construct pinions out of material so light and flexible and yet so strong, and attached to the body by thongs and bands so tenacious, that man might hope to imitate a bird's flight; but all these efforts have ended in broken bones if not broken necks. What is the difficulty? Why cannot a man construct wings to fly with, such as a bird has that enable him to fly and even to rest on the wing? Where the man's wings begin, his life ends, so that his wings are a burden to be borne, not pinions to bear him; but where the bird's wings begin, the bird's life does not end—it penetrates the wings to the utmost tip; those hollow bones are pervaded as it were with the breath of the bird, the muscles with his blood and energy, and so the bird's life reaches to the ends, the feather-tips of the wings, and they are not burdens but pinions. The man's wings are substitutes, the bird's are attributes. So there is no place in the Bible where one can say: "Here the prophetic element begins and there it ends." These predictions are not like a man's wing, but like a bird's wing; the whole Bible is penetrated and permeated by the Spirit of Life, which is the Spirit of Prophecy.

Then again, the Messianic predictions in the Old Testament, occult as well as obvious, latent as well as patent, are the key to the understanding of the Old Testament. When Christ gave that discourse on the way to Emmaus, and when the writer of the Epistle to the Hebrews wrote out what seems to be the substance of that discourse, we obtain a clue to the facts of Old Testament history as a whole. If we knew our Bibles as we shall know them some day, we might find that there is not a narrative, however remote it may seem to be from the person of Jesus Christ, that has not some reference to Him or His work, constructive and destructive—either to His personality or the personality of the Devil; or to the methods by which He advances righteousness, or by which the subtle enemy of God and man promotes unrighteousness. The more the reader is enlightened with a true insight into the Bible, the more he can begin anywhere, opening at random, and preach Jesus, as Philip did to the eunuch.

Dr. A. J. Gordon, of Boston, on one occasion gave to his little children in the nursery a dissected map, somewhat elaborate, and said: "Do not try to put it together in any way excepting the right way, for if you do you will break it." He came back in a few moments, and the map was all put together rightly with its scores of different pieces. "Why," he said, as Isaac said to Jacob, "How hast thou found it so quickly, my son?" His boy said: "Father, there is a man on the back." Sure enough, there was a figure of a man pasted on the back for some advertising purpose, and the children had discovered here a head or foot, and there an eye or ear, and so put the map together. There is a man on the back of the Holy Scriptures, and if all the books of the Old and New Testaments are arranged around the central Person of our Lord, He is found to be the key to the structure of the whole Bible. It is made by this all pervading Presence one Book, one Revelation; He is the one open door into its innermost mysteries.

This is God's way in part of authenticating His own Scriptures. Books from one particular press, made of paper from a particular factory, often show a waterline in the paper which runs through all the leaves and may be seen back of the print, indicating that all came from the same paper mill. When these inspired pages are held up and seen in the light of God, His waterline is found on every page, the outline image of his dearly beloved Son, pervading and explaining the Holy Scriptures. The believer who, in a reverent spirit, studies the Book of God, discovers this image of Jesus Christ stamped on the whole book from beginning to end, woven into its texture.

There is a singular interrelation between all the parts of this book. The student finds himself following the perimeter of a golden ring. Starting, as it were, at the top of the circle, with Adam in Eden, we trace his fall, and the downward course of history to the time of the flood; then still down through the awful apostasy of the race till the lowest point is reached in that most damnable deed—the crucifixion of the Son of God as a malefactor. But in His Resurrection, we begin the ascent on the other half of the circle. Then as we go up we meet the Holy Spirit's outpouring at Pentecost; and so on to the modern period of missions, with the prosecution of a world's evangelisation; and, when the last chapter of Revelation is reached, we are back where we were in the first chapters of Genesis: "The tree of life in the midst of the garden;" "The water of life, clear as crystal;" "The tabernacle of God is with men"— only that, in the original Eden, there came the curse of sin, but, in the new City, "There shall be no more curse." Jesus Christ is the center of this great circle, and to Him as a center, every point in the perimeter of this golden ring is related.

Christ, who is the key to the plan of the Bible, also unlocks God's plan of the ages. In Him is the secret which explains the Book and all history from creation to the new creation and the ultimate redemption. If the Bible be studied with reference to this redemption plan, it records first, the creation of man and his fall; then the selection of a people out of whom Christ is to come, and who are to be the custodians of the inspired prophecies concerning Him; then these holy Oracles, gradually compiled through the ages, constituting the sacred Book of God, to be the guide to His chosen people, and full of Christ from Genesis to Malachi; then comes the record of the period of Christ himself, when the New Man appears on the historic scene, corresponding to Adam at the time of His creation. Then comes the separation from the world of another people, called the "ecclesia" or called out ones, that church to be the new representative in the world of God in Christ, and the custodian of the doctrine of Redemption; then the second part of the book is completed, adding the New Testament to the Old; and finally the glimpse of the kingdom at the end of the dispensation, which is itself the beginning of another epoch and a new creation. This whole redemptive scheme is forecast in the Bible, which God and His Church are working out in history.

Such devout study becomes to those who will undertake it, another Emmaus walk. When with prayerfulness and reverence the Holy Scriptures are examined, we find, as step by step we pass on in our search, Another Who is speaking to us, unfolding and expounding in all the Scriptures the things concerning Himself; and to all such students there comes a time of special blessed, divine revelation, when through the scriptures He makes known Himself, as He made Himself known to those disciples in the breaking of bread. Probably when He lifted those pierced hands to offer a few words of blessing on the food, they saw the prints of the nails. He still continues to take devout disciples into the secret place with Himself, draw aside His disguise and show the marks of the Crucified. Then His humanity no more hides His divinity; even the Crown of Thorns blossoms into a wreath of celestial roses, and appears as the diadem of God upon His brow.

When the late George H. Stuart, Esq., of Philadelphia, had occasion, during the American Civil War, to pass through the lines on an errand of mercy, at night time, a sentinel challenged him: "Give the pass-word." "Washington." "That is not the pass-word." "Very well," he said, "I will go back and rectify the mistake." He had been given the pass-word of the day before. So he returned presently, knowing the pass-word of the day. "Who is there?" "A friend." "The password?" "Advance." "All right, Mr. Stuart," came the response of the sentinel. Coming near he said to the sentinel, "I have given you the pass-word. Do you know God's pass-word to heaven?" "For many years I have known it, Mr. Stuart; it is the name of Jesus." And blessed be God, that password is the same yesterday, to-day, and forever.

CHAPTER VIII

The Bible and Forecasts of Atonement

Russia is a great empire. The heart of Russia is Moscow; the heart of Moscow is the Kremlin; and the heart of the Kremlin is the Treasury, where vacant thrones and crowns, set upon pedestals, represent the conquered provinces of Russia.

The heart of the Bible is Messianic Prophecy; the heart of Messianic Prophecy is the Person of Jesus Christ, and the heart of the Revelation of His Person is Redemption by blood. Hence the importance of carefully tracing the testimony of the Word of God concerning His atoning work.

Among the important words, already referred to, in the Epistle to the Hebrews, are three—"body," "shadow," and "outline" or "image." "Body" represents the substantial reality or verity of which the "outline" or "image" is a delineation, just as a profile or drawing without colour represents a human being. "Shadow" is an outline cast on the ground or elsewhere by the light shining upon the body itself. We read of the "example and shadow of heavenly things;" of a "shadow of

144

things to come, but the body is Christ;" of the "image of those things;" etc.*

The "body" was yet in the distant future, veiled from human sight. In the Old Testament is the profile drawing in outline, without colour, and yet so complete that, when compared with the actual portrait, hung on the walls of the New Testament, filled in with colour, the profile or outline, however ancient, and the fuller image, however recent, are identical—one being but the filling out of the other.

The conception of a "shadow" is suggestive. If any erect object stands where the setting sun shines on it a shadow is produced, at times so lengthened as to reach far toward the opposite horizon. A great Personality fills the New Testament—Jesus Christ the Crucified One—but the lengthened shadow of the crucified Christ extends backward and touches the remotest horizon of history. Thus one long "shadow of things to come," cast backward by the sunlight of God, covers the Old Testament records and periods, and to look at these correspondent facts compels the double conviction of the divine origin of the Scriptures and the divine character of Jesus Christ.

"Atonement" is not a scriptural word, as com-

* Hebrews VIII:5; X:1.

monly used. The Shakespearean sentence, "He seeks to make at-one-ment between the Duke of Gloucester and his brother," is often quoted as giving a definition of "atonement," but it is misleading. The original word, used in the New Testament, means "reconciliation;"* and in the Old Testament it is, as near as may be, the equivalent of *that which covers*—"propitiation." Perhaps the phrase most nearly expressing the sense of the word atonement, as used by orthodox believers, is redemption by blood; and it is to be hoped that the time is far distant when this will be abandoned in concession to the modern demand that the "blood" be eliminated from Christianity.

It is at the peril of our faith that we put on the blood the stigma of reproach. From the first pages of the Bible to the last, blood colours, with its crimson, the entire inspired record. Redemption by blood is the central factor in atonement, as set forth both in the New Testament and in the Old, the connection between which was long since sagaciously expressed by Augustine, that "the Old Testament is patent in the New, and the New is latent in the Old;" that the truths doctrinally and historically set forth in the New Testament, are found pictorially, typically and symbolically, in the

* Romans v:11. καταλλογη.

Old Testament; that while the New unfolds the Old, at the same time the Old enfolds the New.

One example of this may suffice. Of all the epistles of the New Testament, the Epistle to the Romans is conceded to be the fullest and clearest in setting forth the essentials of the doctrine of redemption. The others which follow presuppose this epistle, though it was not the first written; and the providence of God so guided even the compilation of the canon of the New Testament as that the epistles should there be found in the order, not of composition, but of truth as it needed to be progressively taught.

In the Epistle to the Romans, the first eight chapters set forth several leading and distinct truths with regard to redemption.

That which is foremost, as lying at the bottom of the whole scheme of salvation, is that Redemption begins in *deliverance from the wrath of God*—His holy retributive judgment upon sin. (i:18–ii:16.) We are further taught:

(2.) That Redemption provides for *the expiation of the guilt* which invokes and challenges the wrath. (iii:9–24)

(3.) That Redemption *puts away the sin*, removes it from between the sinner and God as something that is cancelled and obliterated. (iii:25–iv:8)

(4.) That Redemption *cancels a debt to the law*, justice and government of God, and makes it as though it had never existed, so that we have pacific relations with a holy God. (IV:8–25.)

(5.) That Redemption involves a *reconciliation* or a *restoration* between the alienated sinner and God, so that he becomes a member of the divine family. (V:1–21.)

(6.) That there is *emancipation from the power of sin*, as there has been deliverance from its penalty. "The law of the spirit of life in Christ Jesus hath made me free from the law of sin and death." (VII:1–VIII:2).

(7.) The grand climax of the eighth chapter reveals the supreme truth of Redemption, that *all this depends upon a personal relation with the Redeemer—the Lord Jesus Christ.* Redemption does not come through a truth taught, nor even through blood shed, apart from vital union with the Person of the Redeemer. He is Himself the Way, the Truth and the Life. Not by any teaching, nor even by any sacrifice, alone, but by identification with Him, are we saved. (VIII:29–39).

It is with the surprise and delight of a new discovery that the student of scripture finds all these same truths set forth, illustratively and pictorially, in the first three books of the Old Testament, and in about the same order as that in which they are unfolded in the Epistle to the Romans. They are found in the Old Testament, not explicitly, but presented as object lessons, or in pictorial representations, in three great feasts or festivals appointed for the Jews. The whole ritual of Judaism is important as a typical forecast of New Testament doctrinal teaching and fully interpreted only thereby; but, for the sake of brevity, we take simply three of these feasts or festivals, all of them connected with the tenth day of the seventh month: the festival of the Passover; the festival of the great Day of Atonement, or Propitiation, and the festival, occurring once in fifty years, known as the Jubilee, which began on the evening of the great Day of Atonement, a fact which itself is typical, for only when the Atonement was completed could the Jubilee year begin.

In the Passover, the main conception is, obviously, "Deliverance from judgment, or wrath—" the leading thought of the Epistle to the Romans: "The wrath of God is revealed from heaven against all ungodliness and unrighteousness of men, who hold the truth in unrighteousness." That is where, as Paul shows, redemption must begin, and in the Feast of the Passover, which began the sacred circle of festivals, such deliverance from wrath is plainly emphasized as the first necessity. When Jehovah and the Destroying Angel passed over every Jewish house, it was because of the blood, sprinkled on the side posts and the upper doorposts,—those who passed out and in being thus surrounded by the blood—and God said, "When I see the blood, I will pass over you, and will not suffer the Destroyer to smite you." The one thought is deliverance from judgment.

The second of these festivals was the great Day of Atonement or Propitiation. Commentators have found here a battleground over the question what is meant by the goat, "*Azazel.*" The simplest sense is ordinarily the safest for, when a dozen theories of biblical interpretation are suggested, that which is most literal, lies most on the surface, is most conformed to common sense and which needs the least philosophy to master it, is usually the true one. God did not make His book for scholars or sages, but for common folks.

The ceremonies on the Day of Atonement were, as near as possible, twin ceremonies; two kids of goats of the same age and size, being chosen, and, as Jewish writers say, the goat, Azazel, distinguished from the other only by a scarlet ribbon or piece of cloth tied to it. One of the two was slain, and the blood poured out; on the other the hands of the High Priest Aaron were heavily laid, as though to transfer to him a heavy load of guilt, while the High Priest confessed over his head, in words still recorded by Jewish writers, his own sins and the sins of the people. Then that goat was led away by the hand of some fit man into a "lone place," out of sight of the people, whence he would not find his way back to the camp. Azazel means "removal," "putting away at a distance," and here is a twin conception: First, of guilt expiated, —and, again, of sin borne away—removed from before the face of God.*

"Removal" is more than expiation. Expiation covers guilt; removal has to do with fellowship; when sin is expiated, as to its guilt, it is practically blotted out as to its record and remembrance; it is put behind God's back; "cast into the depths of the sea;" borne away into the lone place, never to find its way back and bring guilt to remembrance. Disciples often dredge up from the depths of this merciful oblivion the sins that God has buried there, out of sight, not content to let forgiven sin lie, as it ought to lie, in the hidden forgetfulness of His love and grace. And again, those whom He forgives too often say: "I can forgive, but I cannot forget." What if God for-

---

* "The Lord also hath *put away* thy sin"—II Samuel XII: 13.

gave and did not forget? Then, when a praying believer draws near to the throne of grace, even forgiven sin would keep coming up before God and before the suppliant to taint communion and hinder mutual approach. It is perilous to pray, "Forgive us our debts *as we forgive our* debtors," while such is the fashion of our forgiveness. If that Lord's prayer teaches anything, it is that we are to adopt, in dealing with men, the principle that we would have God adopt in dealing with us, which He enjoins on us as our law of dealing with others.

These twin ceremonies therefore set forth this double conception: That the guilt of sin is expiated in the blood of the slain Lamb but, as the dead victim cannot at the same time represent a living presence and a living power, sins are also borne away representatively by the goat, Azazel. We have thus the dying Christ and the living Christ both typified. He Who bore our sins up to the cross to atone for their guilt, also bore them out of sight, to sink them into the depths of the sea of oblivion, so that even the remembrance of them is no more before God. He therefore says: "Their sins and their iniquities *will I remember no more*."

That is a significant phrase with similar meaning—"Blotted out." When the Jewish scribes wrote on wax tablets with the "stylus" (from which our English word "style"), to obliterate the record, it was needful only to turn the stylus round, and with the flat end press back the wax into the cavities, and it was as though there never had been a record. Sin forgiven and forsaken is with God as though it had never been; He puts it away. Hence that strong language used by Paul: "Blotting out the handwriting of ordinances that was against us and contrary to us, and took it out of the way, nailing it to His cross." (Colossians II: 14.) There are two ways of dealing with a debt: to pay it, and to destroy the record of it. The Lord Jesus Christ nailed sin to the cross—that cancelled it as a debt; and he blotted it out—that annihilated it as a record.

In the third Festival, three things took place when the trump of Jubilee sounded:

(1.) All debts were cancelled.*

(2.) All alien estates were restored to their owners.

(3.) Every one involved in servitude, for any cause, was emancipated.

These correspond to the other truths taught in

* It is said that a document, showing debt, was in two parts, and that the creditor brought his portion and nailed it to the doorpost of the debtor's house, and that the debtor brought out his portion and nailed that also beside it to show that the two belonged together, and the debt was cancelled. Compare "Indenture."

the Epistle to the Romans: cancellation of the debt to the law and justice; restoration to God's favour; emancipation from the power as well as penalty of sin.

In the 25th chapter of Leviticus we have a description of the ceremonies and laws of the Jubilee year, and there is a special provision as to the "kinsman," from the 25th to the 30th verses. It is what is known as the "law of the kinsman" (Heb. goël). There are two conditions: first, that the man who undertakes redemption, shall be a kinsman—that is, have kin with the family needing redemption; secondly, he must belong to some other branch of the family, otherwise he would be involved in its calamities, and be unable to act in the capacity of a redeemer.

These provisions are historically illustrated in the book of Ruth. Naomi had lost her husband and her two sons in the forbidden land of Moab, and her estate in the Land of Promise appears to have been in a condition of bankruptcy. We read in Ruth, second chapter, first verse, that "Naomi had a kinsman of her husband, a mighty man of wealth of the family of Elimelech, and his name was Boaz." The name Boaz means, "in him is ability." Boaz, being a kinsman, had the right to redeem, but being of a higher branch of the family, and having wealth, he had also the power to redeem. Thus, what is a precept in Levitical law, finds an historical example in the interposition of Boaz in behalf of Ruth, who was the widow of Mahlon. This narrative, which superficial readers think is only a love story, is susceptible of a deeper interpretation. It is the one and only book of the Old Testament that plainly suggests the necessity that our Redeemer should have a double nature, as the God-Man, in order to fulfil the conditions upon which only, man's redemption can be accomplished. Thirty times in that short book the word "kinsman" is found, or "redeemer," "near kinsman," "next of kin," "kindred"—like words, all having reference to like things. Ruth was a stranger, a Moabitess, who came into the Land of Promise as the widow of an Israelite who had gone into the forbidden land of Moab, and died there. She came as a servant rather than a mistress; a bankrupt through debt on her estate; an alien, not belonging properly to the tribes of Israel. Boaz takes compassion upon her, cancels the debt, brings her out of an alienated condition into the true ancestral line of the Messiah, and not only restores to her Mahlon's lost estate, but emancipates her from a servile condition, and makes her his own wife. That which constituted any man a redeemer in Israel, and gave the right to redeem, as laid down in the Levitical code, is thus historically illustrated in this narrative.

How plainly this book is intended to teach the doctrine concerning Redemption, will be seen by examining chapter four, verses 4–10. Here the word "redemption" occurs five times in a single verse, nine times in three verses, and in the tenth verse, Boaz declares that in redeeming the property he also purchases the widow of Mahlon to be his own wife. Nothing can explain the extreme minuteness of detail here except a typical design on the part of the inspiring Spirit; and, when we turn to the New Testament, the typical meaning is made entirely clear. We find there is presented, as in the first two chapters of the Epistle to the Hebrews, the double nature of the Lord Jesus Christ, which will receive further consideration in a subsequent chapter. We may now anticipate far enough to say that our Lord Jesus Christ had to become one with man in order to have the right to redeem. He is, therefore, our fellowman; but if He had been involved in man's fall, and identified with man's sin, He could not have acted as Redeemer. No sinner can redeem himself, much less can he redeem his brother.* He is, therefore,

* None of them can by any means redeem his brother, nor give to God a ransom for him.—Psa. XLIX: 7.

as the God-man, our Boaz: by that kinship and strength or ability, He is "able to save to the uttermost all that come unto God by Him."

The correspondence between this truth as doctrinally set forth in the New Testament, and pictorially, typically, and historically in the Old, is so close, that we cannot avoid the conviction of a divine design. Here is a new example of the fact that, while the "body" of truth is found in the New Testament, the lengthened "shadow" and "example" of it are found in the Old. Here is an exact outline in the book of Ruth of what is afterward filled in, in the Person and work of the God-man, our Redeemer. Thus, all the leading truths, and essentially in the order of the Epistle to the Romans, are forecast in the three great Festivals of the Jews.

The Passover: Deliverance from wrath by the shedding of blood.

The Day of Atonement, in the expiation of guilt, and putting away of the remembrance of sin.

The Year of Jubilee: Cancellation of debt and deliverance from bankruptcy; Restoration of an alien to the family rights; and emancipation from servitude.

All these are inseparable from the person of the redeemer, whose kinship with the party to be redeemed gives the right to redeem, and whose exemption from such party's calamities, gives the power. Moreover, the redemption, as in the case of Ruth, involves not only the purchase of the inheritance, but the purchase of the original owner. So Jesus Christ, the Redeemer, redeems man by taking him into sacred union with Himself. Whom He saves from their lost estate, He weds as His chosen Bride. And so, Paul, writing of the "great mystery concerning Christ and the Church," represents what He, as Husband, does for the Church: "He loved the Church, and gave Himself for it; He sanctified and cleansed it; He nourishes and cherishes it, and He presents it to Himself.*

Another typical forecast must be referred to before we leave this subject. Five sacrifices or offerings are described and enjoined in the first three chapters of Leviticus, and these are divisible into two classes; First, ill savour offerings; and, second, those of sweet savour: the former were supposed, when burnt, to go downward as something under a curse; the others, to go upward as a sweet savour in the nostrils of God. What the philosophy of all this is, probably an Archangel cannot fully unfold; this is another theme that will bear study for all eternity. But some truth seems

* Ephesians v: 25-33.

to be plainly taught. The word "burnt" is different in the two cases. In one it means "to turn to ashes," and in the other, "to ascend as in flames." This suggests the idea that when a life is forfeited by sin and an innocent victim is laid on the altar in place of the sinner, Justice—like a descending fire—consumes the offering and turns it to ashes; and then the ransomed life, moved by gratitude and adoration by what has been done on its behalf, is voluntarily laid before God, and, by a fire which is not a consuming but a refining fire, aflame with worship, gratitude, affection, that life is swept upward to God as something acceptable in Jesus Christ. Here are suggested,—a descending fire, an ascending flame—something accursed through sin, something approved through redemption.

If we look beyond the first eight chapters of Romans, the second part contains truth complementary to the first. In the first part, the dominant idea is the sacrifice of the innocent for the guilty; in the second, the dominant note is the sacrifice of the ransomed soul to the service of the Ransomer: "I beseech you, therefore, brethren, by the mercies of God, that ye present your bodies a living sacrifice, holy, acceptable unto God, which is your reasonable (spiritual) service."

Here is another double truth taught: a life must

be given for a life in order to redemption and salvation,—the life of the innocent for the guilty; but second, the life of the ransomed must be given to the Ransomer, in order to sanctification and service. These double truths, forecast in the Old Testament, are plainly taught in the New.

Sublimely simple all this is,—and as a matter of fact, a little child can understand this great primary fact and truth of the Word of God, redemption by blood.

The greatest proof, perhaps, that Christianity is from God, is the long historic argument of experiment. Ever since the day when Abel laid his lamb on the altar, and saw, somehow, the coming Seed of the woman, as his Atoning Saviour, down to this very day, the one thing that has proved the salvation of men has been faith in the Lord Jesus Christ. No man can show, in all infidel theories, in all agnostic negations, in all sceptical notions, in all refining away of the Doctrine of Atonement, anything that can bring to believers what this doctrine has brought to them for the last two thousand years, and those who trust in Christ may well refuse to turn aside to consider the abandonment of this confidence until something better is offered in its place.

Primary truths, like these, are the heart of the

whole Word of God, and the rock basis of the history of the Church of God. The argument from experiment is indubitable and unanswerable. The world can furnish nothing else that saves, nothing that sanctifies, nothing that removes the sense of guilt and alienation from God, nothing that brings into communion with the unseen world and the unseen God, and keeps the soul, even in the dying hour, confident, and enables one to say triumphantly

"In my hand no price I bring,
Simply to Thy cross I cling."

It is worth while to have something to cling to and rest upon in a dying hour, instead of making a leap in the dark.

Many of the great men of Britain have been eminent also as men of God. Bishop Butler, who was called the Melchisedec of the "English Church," —because he had no predecessor and no successor— fell into great depression in his dying moments, and he said: "Chaplain, where shall I find hope? Where shall I find a solid resting place for my poor feet?" "My Lord Bishop, Jesus died for you," he answered. "How shall I know that He died for *me?* How shall I get hold of it for myself?" And the Chaplain answered: "Him that cometh unto me,

I will in no wise cast out." "That is just what I wanted," said the dying Bishop.

Archbishop Benson used to say that the primary truths are proofs of the divine character of the Bible, because "a little child can comprehend primary truths, and many people cannot get hold of anything beyond them; while the greatest must come back from all their excursions into philosophy and science to rest at last upon them." "Jesus died for me," Charles Haddon Spurgeon declared to be the four words he had lived by, and was going to die by.

When they asked the dying Faraday: "What are your speculations?" he replied that he was not pillowing his head upon any "speculations." "I know whom I have believed, and am persuaded that He is able to keep that which I have committed to Him, against that day."

The late Lord Bishop of Durham, one of the grandest men ever in the English Church, having at the last a comparatively long and painless illness, some thought he must be meditating some new work of scholarship, and ventured to ask. "No," he said, "I am coming back from all my studies to remember that Jesus died for me. I take two or three great primary truths and dwell on them."

So much for the testimonies of the great. Let us come down now to the lowest level.

In Southampton, some years ago, there was an adulterer, a blasphemer, a profane swearer, the terror of the whole district. He ventured into a tent one night, on the last day of a mission, and heard a sermon on "Him that cometh unto Me, I will in no wise cast out." He said: "If there is any salvation for such a wretch as I am, I want it." And he stayed and talked with the preacher afterward, and immediately gave himself to God, and began a new life. He let alone his drink and tobacco, and all his vile habits, and was the admiration of the district where he had been the terror before. One night he was knocked down by a passing train and both his legs were cut off at the thigh. When the surgeon told him, "I am sorry to say it, but, my dear fellow, you have not more than fifteen minutes to live," he began to sing:

"Hallelujah, 'tis done, I believe on the Son,
I'm saved by the blood of the Crucified One."

The Gospel that can save such a man as that, and make him happy in view of death, fifteen minutes later, is a great deal better than anything that agnosticism, skepticism, or infidelity can bring him.

Yes, it is the Gospel for the little ones of earth. The poor Scotch lad, half-imbecile, who wanted to come to the Lord's Table, but was thought by the minister of the kirk to have really not enough intelligence to discern the Lord's body, as he turned away, was heard, as he went out of the door, to say with sobs in his simple fashion:

"Three in One, and One in Three,
And the Middle One, He died for me."

CHAPTER IX

THE BIBLE AND THE BLOOD

THE PHILOSOPHY OF THE ATONEMENT

FROM the *fact* of the atonement, we turn now to look at some indications of God's *plan* in the atonement, or the philosophy of the plan of salvation.

Three rules of Scripture study are of great importance and consequence: Search, Meditate, Compare. *Search*, because the truth in Holy Scripture lies often under the surface. "The letter killeth, but the spirit giveth life." That which is in the Scriptures for our highest education, instruction and consolation, is not superficially to be picked up or gleaned; it has to be dug for, like veins of gold that yield only to the pickaxe. *Meditation* is bringing the whole nature, mind and heart, sensibilities, conscience and will, into such a prayerful and receptive frame, as to open up the entire being to the illumination of the Spirit. *Comparison* is that of which particularly this chapter treats, putting scripture teachings side by side that each may throw light on the other.

While the Bible does not present truth, crystallized into a system, it does contain truth in substance, and furnish material for a system—not as stone in the structure, but as stone in the quarry. The value of thus collating, and comparing spiritual things with spiritual, is found in the constant discovery of unsuspected correspondences, coincidences, and mutual adaptations. The stone is found to be hewn and shapen, ready to be carried to the site of the building, and there put together without the need of axe, or any iron tool to adjust the various blocks to their decreed place; so that one is enabled to build up a system of truth, out of Biblical materials, and according to what is evidently a preconceived divine plan.

A mythical story is told of Michael Angelo and "The Sleeping Cupid," that he dug up, in different localities, certain fragments of the sculptor's chisel, which, being put together, proved to be all parts of one original statue, broken and scattered in the time of revolution and war. In some such way, those who search the Holy Scriptures, meditate upon them, and compare spiritual things with spiritual, often reach surprising results.

It becomes us to tread with unsandalled feet on ground so holy as the philosophy of the atonement, searching the scriptures, if haply we may find there any indications that God Himself has given of the principles that underlie atonement for sin. Some of the problems that confronted God with regard to man's redemption, we can scarcely understand at all because of sensibilities dulled by habitual contact with evil. Familiarity with sin involves the loss of all true conception of its enormity and deformity. Yet there can be no high value placed upon the work of Christ until there is some apprehension of the desperation and degradation of man's fallen state, and the utter corruption of his nature.

There are several aspects of sin which, obviously, must be considered and met in a redemptive plan, and which, in part, have already been considered:

Sin is transgression, and transgression demands penalty.

Sin is guilt, and guilt demands expiation.

Sin is character, and character demands renewal.

Sin is slavery, and slavery demands emancipation.

Sin is ruin, and ruin demands rebuilding.

Sin is war against Almighty God, and this demands the vindication of God's honour and holiness. There must be on His part no complicity with sin, in a lax fashion of pardoning.

These are a few indications of the tremendous moral problems that confronted the great Lawgiver. Nothing short of Infinite Wisdom and Infinite Love were equal to forming a scheme that should at once save the sinner from sin, and save God from compromise and complicity with it.

In the Bible at least a few intimations are given as to the way in which all these necessary factors in the problem were met.

First, sin is transgression of the law. "Who His Own Self bare our sins in His Own Body on the tree." "Whom God hath set forth to be a propitiation through faith in His blood, to declare His righteousness for the remission of sins that are past, through the forbearance of God."

Again, sin is guilt, and guilt must be expiated: "The blood of Jesus Christ His Son cleanseth us from all sin."

And, again, sin is character; it involves the nature: "Except a man be born from above, he cannot see the kingdom of God." "If any man be in Christ, he is a new creation. Old things are passed away; behold all things are become new."

Sin is slavery: "The law of the Spirit of life in Christ Jesus hath made me free from the law of sin and death." "Stand fast, therefore, in the liberty wherewith Christ hath made you free, and be not entangled again in the yoke of bond-age."

Sin is ruin: "For this purpose the Son of God was manifested, that He might destroy (or undo) the works of the Devil."

And, finally, sin is war against Almighty God, and God has no complicity with the enmity of the sinner against Him and His government; and we read, in that crowning verse in the third of Romans: "To declare, I say, His righteousness, that He might be just, and the Justifier of him that be-lieveth in Jesus." God declares all the great ends sought in redemption to be fulfilled in His plan of Salvation.

Perhaps some further hints may be found as to the way in which those ends are fulfilled, by first inquiring as to the basal conceptions, lying at the foundation of redemption.

First of all, there must be a legal satisfaction to a broken law. A death penalty was attached to sin, from the beginning: "The soul that sinneth, it shall die," crystallizes in proverbial form that first threat and warning: "In the day that thou eatest thereof, dying, thou shalt die." Here we touch the basis of the whole system, both of retribution and redemption. The broken law of God must be honoured and maintained; the death penalty must be executed; there must be satisfaction to the principles of divine justice, law and government. Upon the upholding of the sanctions of the law, all government ultimately depends both for its purity and permanency.

Secondly, such satisfaction is provided by substitution. Some are needlessly afraid of that word, substitution; yet, redemption, as taught in the Bible, is certainly based on this principle,— an innocent victim takes the place of the guilty— a penalty is borne vicariously to vindicate law and justice; the offending party, through the substitution of a life for a life, escaping that eternal death which would otherwise have been his portion. From the first hint of this redemptive scheme, in the earlier books of the Bible, the careful reader may trace, from Abel's altar on, this principle of substitution systematically carried out. The first martyr came to God, bringing a lamb from his flock, and offering that lamb as a sacrifice for sin. Thus understood, Abel's offering affords the most satisfactory explanation of the language used by God to Cain, when his "countenance fell:" "Why is thy countenance fallen? If thou doest well, shalt not thou be accepted? And if thou doest not well, behold, the sin-offering croucheth at the door." i. e., a sin offering avails for you as for Abel; and you may, in the same way, "be accepted" by the substitution of the innocent victim for the guilty sinner." In the offering of the Paschal Lamb, and on the great Day of Atonement, the same essential and important lesson is explicitly taught.

Yet further on in the Old Testament, we are taught that redemption is not only by satisfaction to a broken law, and by substitution of the innocent for the guilty, but that it is on the principle of representation which is a step in advance even of substitution.* Though these terms are not scriptural, they answer the purpose, as equivalents, briefly to convey or express the scriptural truth.

The principle of representation is first clearly enunciated in Exodus XXVIII: 38–43, a passage so significant as especially to need study.

Aaron—undoubtedly the typical representative of the great High Priest that has passed into the heavens—is bidden, when he comes into the holiest place of all, to wear, bound upon the forefront of the mitre, the holy crown with the inscription, "Holiness to the Lord," indicating absolute surrender to God and perfect holiness, realized of

* Isaiah LIII.

course only in his great anti-type, Jesus Christ himself. The thirty-eighth verse reads: "And it shall be always upon his forehead, that they (the people, the children of Israel) may be accepted before the Lord." Very significant is this change of pronouns.: "always upon *his* forehead, that *they* may be accepted." As he goes into the Holy of Holies, he represents the people. Christ, the great High Priest of whom Aaron was only the type, goes into the Holiest of all, "appearing in the very presence of God for us," and His Holiness, which is always before the face of God, is the ground of the acceptance of all believers; His presence before God being perpetual, that their acceptance with God may be equally perpetual.

The forty-third verse of this same chapter presents the complimentary truth, that, if they, the parties so represented, failed to conform to the regulations which God had established, they should "bear their *own* iniquity and die for it." Here is the dread alternative. The sinner who rejects the substitution, satisfaction and representation of Jesus Christ, bears his own iniquity and dies for it. But he who takes refuge in Jesus Christ is "accepted in the beloved," and the perfection of his Substitute is the perpetual pledge of his own acceptance. Such provisions of grace are surpassingly wonderful!

Still further on, a thought additional to all the rest, is presented—that this redemption is inseparable from regeneration. The Holy Spirit of God supplements and complements the atoning work of Jesus Christ on the cross—Christ expiating penalty, and cleansing guilt; the Holy Spirit, changing the very nature, and so implanting the germ of a holy character. Not only an imputed righteousness, but an imparted righteousness, belongs to the scheme of redemption: first, the believer is, through Jesus Christ, clothed with God's righteousness, as a garment, displacing his own "righteousnesses which are as filthy rags;" and then, underneath this garment of a vicarious righteousness, the Holy Ghost divinely works in the believer, both to will and to do, so that a divine righteousness, in a sense, becomes his own possession; and when he finally appears before the glory of God, and the searching eye of Omniscience falls upon him, and the light more piercing than all other that ever shone, beats upon him like the sun in noontide splendour, even God Himself shall see no spot nor wrinkle nor blemish nor anything rebukable or reprovable in His sight.* Such

* Compare Colossians 1: 22. Jude 24.

173

final perfection for a penitent and believing sinner
would be incredible but for the declaration of the
Lord Himself.

God does not, therefore, simply pardon a sinner,
passing over his sin and guilt because of a redemption by blood, but He recreates the sinner into a
saint; and so, far from setting a premium on sin
by a lax exercise of mercy, He actually regenerates,
renews, recreates in His own image.

There is still another level of redemption, higher,
if possible, than this; for the scheme of salvation which starts with satisfaction and proceeds to substitution, then to representation, and
then to regeneration, ends and is consummated
in eternal identification with the Redeemer.

Identification means being made one with
another. Christ came down from heaven to be
so far made one with the sinner in his sin, as to be
entitled to take his place before the broken law; then
He went back to heaven to take the believing sinner
up with Him as a saint, and seat him with Himself
on the throne. The Bible teaches this double
identification; God becoming man, that He may
be identified with man, and that, in the end, man
may be identified with Him—Christ taking human
nature, that He may bear man's sins and expiate
man's guilt: Christ imparting divine nature to

man that man may be forever sharer both of His holiness and of His happiness. Character ultimately makes condition.

These outlines of God's redemption plan only touch as on the outskirts of one of the greatest themes of which the Word of God treats, the dimensions of which no human or angelic intelligence has ever yet measured or explored.* They suffice, however, to hint the great foundation principles which underlie the whole system of redemption. A few practical inferences may show the bearings of these great truths.

In the study of this subject the question naturally arises whether the moral ends of punishment are met and satisfied in such vicarious atonement. We need to ask, therefore, another preliminary question as to what the moral ends of punishment are; and all will agree that they are somewhat as follows:

(1.) Law, as a broken code, must be honoured and magnified by due infliction of penalty.

(2.) Guilt, as guilt, must be exhibited in its enormity and deformity.

(3.) The sanctions of government must be so upheld that none may sin with impunity.

* 1 Peter 1: 10-12.

(4.) So far as possible, forgiven offenders must be reclaimed and reformed.

(5.) Other offenders must be deterred from similar offences.

(6.) God Himself must be vindicated as an absolutely holy God.

These points, indicated already at the outset of this discussion, in somewhat different terms, are here restated because of their bearing on the question now before us, whether the atonement, redemption by blood, based on the principles of satisfaction, substitution, representation, regeneration, identification—answers the moral ends aimed at in the punishment of sin.

There seems to be no ground for doubt that in the cross of Jesus Christ such manifestation was made of the majesty, perfection, righteousness and inviolability of the law of God, that the universe of intelligent beings saw, and yet shall see, far more, the infinite perfection of that law, and its inviolability—the impossibility of transgressing it without the exaction of penalty. The exhibition to the universe of the essential corruption and guilt of sin, was probably greater, when on the cross God's own Son died for sin, than though every individual transgressor had suffered the full penalty in his own person. Punishment does not in any circumstances necessarily reform offenders,* but millions of such offenders have already been melted into contrition before the cross of Jesus Christ, in whom nothing else had ever awakened penitence. Other millions of believers, on earth to-day, and more numerous than ever before, owe all that they are to that cross. In heathen lands, where no force of law, however stringent, or government, however despotic, where neither prison cell nor rack of torture, could compel men to abandon their evil doing, the most abandoned sinners have bowed before the cross of Christ, subdued and transformed, and this miracle is still going on.

As to the deterring of other offenders, no one can say—so narrow are the limits of our knowledge in this life—what the cross of Christ may have to do with other worlds, possibly peopled by beings exposed to all the moral liabilities of sin, in restraining them from disobedience.

As to the vindication of God's character from all complicity with sin, when He surrendered His Son to the cross for sinners, it was an unspeakable testimony to the fact that, with His deepest nature—the inmost heart of His Deity—He hated with eternal and unchangeable abhorrence, even the

---

* They gnawed their tongues for pain, and blasphemed the God of heaven. Rev. xvi:10.

thought of evil. We grant that vicarious atonement would be immoral, and so impossible, were the substitution compulsory; but it was voluntary, as well as vicarious. The Son of God was not compelled or constrained, even by the will or authority of the Father, unwillingly to take up and bear the cross. He "offered Himself unto God"—a Lamb without spot—as a sacrifice for men. Love's authority was the only constraint. He was driven to Calvary by no decree, but drawn by infinite sympathy and pity.

The principle of substitution is not absolutely new. In human society it has always been an admitted principle; as, for instance, in war. The story of the Napoleonic campaigns is familiar to all, how in the early wars a man was drafted, in France, and, being unable to go to the field himself, hired a substitute and paid a good price for him, who went to the war, and fell on one of the battle-fields. In a subsequent draft, the same man was drafted again. He went to the recruiting office and produced his papers, proving that he had hired and paid for a substitute, who had died on the field; and the entry was accordingly made against his name: "Died in the person of his substitute on the battlefield of Rivoli." The believer, standing before a violated law, as one who has found in

Philosophy of Atonement

Jesus Christ his Substitute, may claim immunity from the desert of his sin; he may boldly affirm, "I died in the person of the Lord Jesus Christ, on the battlefield of Calvary, over eighteen hundred years ago.* That is salvation. That is redemption.

In America a story is told of a well known teacher of boys, in whose school the pupils themselves made rules for their own government, and attached to them what penalties they thought fit. One little fellow, however, more than once violated the law, and became liable to a flogging. He was called up, according to the rules of the boys themselves, to have the rod laid on his back. Just then the door of the school opened, and in came his elder brother, who, taking in the whole situation at a glance, said to the master: "Would you have any objection to my taking the whipping for my brother?" "Do you think, boys, the honour of the school and its laws would be sufficiently upheld?" was the teacher's appeal. They held up their hands, whereupon the brother bared his back and took the whipping instead of the offender. The principle of substitution was again illustrated.

Another touching story is told, as to the war between Russia and Circassia in the middle of the last century. The prophet chief Schamyl, almost

* II Cor. v:15; Rom. vi:1-8.

adored by his followers, found that some one was exposing to the enemy his designs and plans; and he made a decree, which he promulgated to his followers, that if the traitor were found out, one hundred lashes on the bare back should be administered for the offence. A few days later, it was discovered, to his astonishment, that the guilty party was *his own mother*. He went into fasting and retirement for two days, and coming out, pallid and ghastly, ordered his mother to be brought from the tent and her back bared for the scourge. He stood by while one, two, three, four, five of those fearful lashes gashed her flesh; then he bade the executioner arrest his blows, bared his own back, and took the other ninety-five lashes on his own person, till the flesh hung in shreds. The effect, it is said, was electric—his followers were melted, and even his mother was utterly subdued, as she could never have been by mere force. This exhibition of vicarious love and of the principle of substitution and satisfaction, accomplished all desirable ends more effectively than the full penalty executed on the offender.

Thus the principle of substitution is not entirely foreign to humanity, and the beauty and power of it have been many a time acknowledged even in the circles of society. Neither is the principle of representation absolutely new. Certainly those who live under a constitutional government and have a congress or a parliament to which they elect members, ought to understand that principle as a very common one. A man sent to a legislature from any district is called a representative, because his views and acts are supposed to represent his constituency. If they find otherwise, and he does not vote according to their convictions and will, they displace him by another. The principle of representation is that someone shall be appointed by mutual consent to take another's place. God appoints Jesus Christ to take the place of pentitent, believing sinners. They joyfully consent, and His acts become their acts, His obedience their obedience, His suffering their suffering. Their sin He represents, and atones for it. Their imperfection He represents, and makes up for it by His perfection, so that they are accepted in the Beloved, and for the Beloved's sake. That is the principle of representation. Though it will be referred to, subsequently, it belongs to the matter now under consideration.

As to the principle of identification, in the Bible, as we have seen, the identification of the Redeemer with the redeemed is represented under the figure of the marriage bond. There being no identity so complete as that between husband and wife in the ideal marital relation, God employs this to express Christ's identification with the believer, both in the Old Testament and in the New. It is hinted in the first chapter of Genesis. When Adam fell asleep, and from the rib taken out of his side, God made the woman, and brought her to the man to be his "counterpart," as the Hebrew expresses it, it was the forecast of the Church as taken out of the wounded side of Jesus Christ, bone of His bone, flesh of His flesh, to be His bride. This is a double identification; for when a man weds a woman, the woman marries the man; and he is her husband no more truly than she is his wife; there cannot be a onesided identification. If Christ is the bridegroom of the Church, the Church is the bride of Christ and, hence, where He is, she must be; His glory must be her glory; and His eternal home must be her eternal home.

CHAPTER X

THE BIBLE AND THE GOD-MAN

THE person of the God-Man is the central figure of Biblical revelation. This theme we approach only with the deepest reverence, humility, and sense of ignorance and inadequacy. Of all the truths revealed in the Word of God, this, perhaps, surpasses the rest in grandeur and importance, as a disclosure of the divine philosophy of salvation.

We are told, in the Epistle to the Ephesians, that the mystery of Christ, which in other ages was hidden from the sons of men, was especially revealed to Paul; indeed, he seems to have had unveiled to him some seven mysteries of which he alone treats in his various Epistles. The greatest of all these mysteries, in reference to redemption, is presented in fullness only in the first two chapters of the Epistle to the Hebrews,* and in these two chapters some particular verses are of special importance:

Chapter I: 1. God, who at sundry times and

---

* Perhaps the greatest argument for a Pauline authorship of this epistle.

in divers manners, spake in time past unto the
fathers by the prophets,

2. Hath in these last days spoken unto us by
His Son, whom He hath appointed heir of all
things, by whom also He made the worlds;

3. Who being the brightness of His glory, and
the express image of His person, and upholding
all things by the word of His power, when He
had by Himself purged our sins, sat down on the
right hand of the Majesty on high;

4. Being made so much better than the angels,
as He hath by inheritance obtained a more excel-
lent name than they.

Chap. II: 6. But one in a certain place testified,
saying, What is man, that thou art mindful of him?
or the son of man, that thou visitest him?

7. Thou madest Him a little lower than the
angels; thou crownedst Him with glory and
honour, and didst set Him over the works of thy
hands:

8. Thou hast put all things in subjection under
His feet. For in that He put all in subjection
under Him, he left nothing that is not put under
Him;

9. But we see Jesus, who was made a little
lower than the angels, for the suffering of death,

crowned with glory and honour: that He by the grace of God should taste death for every man.

And then from the 14th verse to the end:

14. Forasmuch then as the children are partakers of flesh and blood, He also Himself likewise took part of the same; that through death He might destroy him that had the power of death, that is, the devil;

15. And deliver them who through fear of death were all their lifetime subject to bondage.

16. For verily He took not on Him the nature of angels (or, "laid not hold upon angels"); but He took on Him (or "laid hold of") the seed of Abraham:

17. Wherefore in all things it behooved Him to be made like unto His brethren, that He might be a merciful and faithful high priest in things pertaining to God, to make reconciliation for the sins of the people:

18. For in that He himself hath suffered being tempted, he is able to succour them that are tempted.

In examining this theme of the God-Man, these thirteen verses need to be kept in mind. The first four affirm unequivocally seven facts which prove that Christ was the Son of God; then seven other facts are specified in the second chapter, which prove that he was equally the Son of Man. There is no attempt to reconcile the apparent paradox; the two aspects of this duality are put before us, the two natures, combined in one personality as they never have been before, and never will be again,—constituting Him a wholly unique person The very grandeur and uniqueness of the conception forbid that it should have proceeded from man; it is a coin having the stamp of the heavenly mint upon it, the image and superscription of God.

A "mystery," in New Testament usage, is a sacred secret, long kept hidden, and, while so hidden, absolutely impenetrable by man; a secret, however, now revealed by the Holy Spirit of God, but only to the initiated, that is, to those who learn God's method of solution or interpretation. There is a chamber of Mystery, containing priceless and unknown treasures, whose door no man can, of himself, unlock, but to which God has given a key; and he who reverently uses it enters into and explores the wonders that are within. Such is the Bible idea of a mystery—an open secret to all believers who are ready to be taught and led of the Spirit of God. This was Bunyan's thought in his "House of the Interpreter."

The consummate mystery of the God-Man cannot be explained by man. Of course not; if it could, it would cease to be a divine mystery, having the stamp of the inscrutable God upon it.

Both the divine and the human aspects of the God-Man are here plainly presented, each as absolutely beyond a doubt.

(1.) In the first place, Christ was the final mouth-piece of God. God had spoken before in the prophets of old time, but the last of His utterances, and the greatest of them, were through Jesus Christ, as the Word of God, the very embodiment of His thought.

(2.) Christ is the universal Heir. All God's possessions are Christ's possessions also, and none others can get any part in the possessions of God except as "joint heirs" with Him, the Universal Heir.

(3.) He was the Creator of the worlds. "By whom He also made the worlds." The word is "Ages," and the idea is that the whole of the temporal order is due to Jesus Christ, who has formed it and framed it for the glory of redemption.

(4.) He was the effulgence of the glory of God; as closely related to God as the light is to the sun: "In the beginning was the Word, and the Word was with God, and the Word was God." In the beginning was the light, and the light was with the sun, and the light was the sun.   He is the very shining of God, the effulgence of His glory.

(5.) "The express image of His person." God is an invisible Spirit; once for all the Godhead has taken a visible form, and that visible form is Jesus Christ, who is as closely related to God as the body is to the soul that inhabits it, and is manifested through it.

(6.) Again, "Upholding all things by the Word of His power."   Not only is Christ the Creator, but the Upholder and Sustainer of the whole temporal order, which would, therefore, fall into absolute ruin but for His upholding word of power.

(7.) Last of all, "He sat down on the right hand of the Majesty on High," Joint Sovereign, with God, of the Universe.

These are the seven proofs of His divinity.   He is as closely linked with God as a word is with the thought it expresses; as a body is with the soul that inhabits it; as light is with the orb that radiates it forth; as an heir is with the owner who transfers to him all his property.   There is no mistaking this teaching, and those who do not believe in the deity of Christ, might as well burn their Bibles, unless they can eliminate this Epistle to the Hebrews.

Equally strong statements are made as to Christ's humanity:

(1.) He came down to man's level, made "a little lower than the angels."

(2.) He took man's nature without its sinfulness; He became properly and perfectly man: "Took on Him the seed of Abraham."

(3.) He suffered man's temptations that He might become the succourer of tempted souls.

(4.) He "tasted death for every man," and by Himself, incapable of sin, "purged our sins."

(5.) He made all believing saints to be one mystical body with Himself. "For both He that sanctifieth and they who are sanctified are all of one." That language cannot be mistaken.

(6.) He destroyed "Him that had the Power of Death"—man's mortal enemy, the devil.

(7.) And last, He restores to humanity the sceptre which was lost in the fall of Adam, so that the eighth Psalm is fulfilled in Jesus Christ.

Here are equally plain indications and affirmations of Christ's perfect humanity, as before of His perfect divinity; so that in this scripture there is presented a unique being, absolutely God, absolutely man, yet uniting the divine and the human natures in one proper personality.

What was the problem presented by man's fall?

Man was created with prophetic intuition of God's will, with priestly right to God's fellowship, and with kingly exercise of sovereignty like unto God Himself. The devil had occupied a supernal position as an angel, possibly an archangel like Gabriel and Michael, but fell from his high position and descended to the lowest depths, the infernal. When man was created and put upon this planet, with his prophetic privileges, his priestly access to God, and his sovereignty and dominion, the devil, envious of man's position, came up from the infernal level to the earthly or terrestrial level, and, presenting subtle temptations before our first parents, accomplished their fall. The consequence was (1), that man lost the proper gift of eternal life, which is something far beyond mere immortality; (2), he lost his liberty as a son of God, and became a slave of the devil; (3), he lost his sovereignty, the devil, by right of conquest, seizing his sceptre of dominion over the earth, and becoming the God of this world.

In order to repair and restore the ruin of the fall, eternal life must somehow be given back to man, his slavery exchanged for liberty, and his lost sceptre of dominion wrested from the hands of the devil and restored to the hands of man.

That was the problem of redemption. How did

God answer and fulfil the conditions of that
problem? We are told most fully in the two
chapters now before us.

It was necessary, in God's plan, that there
should be a second representative of the race.
The first representative had fallen, and in him the
race had sunk hopelessly, and the only way to
redeem mankind was to give the race, as such, a
new opportunity, a new probation; and so a
second representative man was needed, to stand
where Adam stood, undergo similar temptations,
and overcome where man was overcome.

It is conceivable that God might have permitted
a second man to take the place of the first Adam,
and try if he could wrest the sceptre out of the
devil's hands and regain it for the race; but, in
such a case, a man would have been pitted against
a fallen angel, and, as the first man fell before the
subtle wiles of the devil, so might another fall who
attempted to represent the race, and then the
conditions would be worse and more hopeless than
ever.

It is conceivable also that an angel might have
been permitted by God to identify himself with the
human race, become a son of man and undertake
to stand as the race's representative; but this
would imply a struggle between an unfallen and a

fallen angel, and should the angelic man fall under the temptation of the devil, the second experiment would end only in failure.

There was one Being who could stand for man, and who was able to cope with all the powers, lies and wiles of the devil, and that was the Son of God. He undertook to become Man, that being identified with man He might have the right to stand in his place as his representative; yet being identified, on the other hand, with God, He was too mighty for Satan to overcome, and so He undertook that work of redemption to which neither man nor angel was equal.

Just what He did, though all this pertains to the deepest things of God, is revealed here, the key, at least, being given in this Epistle. He undertook to taste death for every man, and to purge away sins in behalf of a fallen race.

In the God-Man is again suggested that idea or representation, already found to be a necessary factor in the redemption scheme. In this passage in Hebrews, more light is thrown upon this particular theme than from any other one scriptural point of view. We are wont to think of the Lord Jesus Christ as the representative of the whole body of believers—what is called His mystical body—the Church. This is grandly true; but the question often arises whether, as the Second Man, His representation reaches any further than the redeemed Church. He is called, in the fifteenth chapter of I Corinthians, both "the Second Man" and the "Last Adam." The Second Man, because there was a first, before Him; the Last Adam, because there shall be none after Him. When this fact of a larger representation of the Adamic race is first brought out clearly in the fifth chapter of Romans, we read: "Nevertheless, death reigned from Adam to Moses, even over them that had not sinned after the similitude of Adam's transgression, who is the figure of Him that is to come ('the figure of the Coming One')" Thus the first time that Adam, as the first man, is explicitly declared to be the figure of Jesus Christ as the Coming One, the Second Man, the Last Adam, it is in immediate connection with the statement that death had reigned even over those who had not sinned after the similitude of Adam's transgression. The Holy Spirit makes no mistakes. There must be some reason why that conception of Christ, as the New Head of the Adamic Race, should be first brought clearly to view in the New Testament, as having some bearing on the mystery of the reign of death over so many that had not sinned after the similitude of Adam's transgression. Jesus Christ is declared to be "the Saviour of all men, especially of those that believe;"* and again to be "the propitiation for our sins; and not for ours only, but also for the whole world."†

This is no field for idle and profitless speculation; but it would appear that, in some sense, Jesus Christ represents, not only the redeemed believing Church, but the world of humanity, the race of Adam. What that representation is, we now inquire. Peradventure these scriptural hints may help to an answer.

The key-note is doubtless given in this fifth chapter of Romans, in the very sentence already quoted: "Death reigned from Adam to Moses even *over them that had not sinned after the similitude of Adam's transgression*." Thousands and millions of little children died then, as now, before the period of intelligent moral agency, and, therefore, before they could intelligently and voluntarily sin after the similitude of Adam's transgression,—before they could either know God's law, or, knowingly, violate it. What became of their departed spirits? Is it conceivable that they were consigned to hell? But, if they were admitted to heaven, it must be through the atoning work of Christ, otherwise there would be human beings in

* I Timothy iv:10.   † I John ii:2. See Greek.

194

heaven that come there without connection with the atonement; but, if they are there through His mediatorial work, it must be on the principle of this new Adamic representation. Beside these millions of infant children, other millions, not children in years, never reach the age of moral responsibility,—imbeciles, idiots, and others whom God sees not to be morally responsible or accountable, for reasons of which we know nothing, and of which He alone can judge. If they are saved, as all of us believe, must it not be likewise through this wider representation of the whole race in this Second Man? All disciples hold a sort of unwritten belief that such are saved, and that, on the ground of Christ's work, those who have not sinned after the similitude of Adam's transgression may be saved without the similitude of Adam's faith. In other words, that, so far as the offspring of Adam have fallen only generically in him, they rise absolutely in Christ; but, when they individually fall, for themselves, by voluntary sin, they must rise, for themselves, that is, in connection with the exercise of voluntary faith. That unformulated creed seems to accord with the doctrine of Holy Scriptures; and, if this construction be correct, the divine philosophy of salvation makes provision for the salvation of little children and all other irresponsible descendants of Adam who die without having sinned after the similitude of his transgression.

Some speculative theologians have argued that the whole race were present in spirit and actually participated in Adam's sin. If so, no one has certainly any recollection of it. The fact is, human philosophy and theology utterly fail to solve this great enigma; but a view seems to be presented here which is open to no objection, and solves the problem. God extended no mercy to fallen angels; they appear to have had no redeemer or offer of redemption; possibly, because each fell for himself, there being no family relationship, involving unborn generations. But His love yearned over the unborn children of Adam, who would inherit the consequences of his sin without sharing its guilt; and, immediately after his sin and fall, God graciously gave the first promise of redemption,—that the Seed of the woman should bruise the serpent's head.

In St. Andrew's, Scotland, an epitaph in the churchyard both evidences and expresses the substance of this belief and hope as held by our ancestors, that Christ was, in some sense, a representative of the whole race, and that many, alike incapable of voluntary transgression or voluntary faith, reach heaven through His death:

"Bold Infidelity, turn pale and die,
  Beneath this stone four infants' ashes lie;
      Say, are they lost or saved?
  If death's by sin, they've sinned, for they are here;
  If heaven's by works, in heaven they can't appear.
      Reason.   Oh, how depraved.
  Turn to the Bible's sacred page, the knot's untied,
  They died, for Adam sinned; they live, for Jesus
      died."

We are taught that, in order to share man's suffering, sorrow and temptation, in order to be made "sin for us" and a "curse" in man's behalf, the Son of God must become man, for only as man could He die; but it was equally necessary that He should not remain under the power of death, for as the Son of God, He was the Prince of Life and could not die, but had a deathless life.   Therefore, great as the mystery is, He became man that He might suffer death for man, but being the Son of God, He could not, even as to His humanity, be holden under the power of death; and so resurrection from the dead, and ascension to the right hand of the throne of God, were the natural and necessary return of the Son of God to His own place in heaven and on the throne. Thus a wonderful work was wrought for man. The fall brought death here, and, after death, a second death, beyond which is no life; but the Son of God came to give the believer life here, and life hereafter, and beyond that life, no death. The exact reversal of all the previous conditions was possible through the finished work of the Lord Jesus Christ.

The climax of this mystery is reached, however, only in identification, which is a double fact; for, if Christ were identified with man, man must be correspondingly identified with Christ. There cannot be a one-sided identity. By as much as a husband belongs to a wife, she belongs to him; and by as much as Christ became one with man, by so much did man become one with Christ. This is the crowning conception that the whole revealed scheme of redemption puts before us.

Had a second man been permitted to stand for the race, and had conquered him by whom the first man was conquered, he could have done nothing more than put man back where he was when he fell, restoring him to a terrestrial level of sovereignty and dominion. If an angel had become one with man, and had overcome Satan in man's behalf, all he could have done would have been to lift man at best to an angelic level. But, when the Son of God became man, and identified man with Himself, and overcame the devil, it was inevitable that He should lift the believer, past the human and angelic, to a divine level. Such is the teaching of this very Scripture. The chapter that demonstrates that Christ was more than an angel, infinitely lifted above the highest angelic ranks, tells us at the close, that the angels are all ministering spirits sent forth to minister to them that shall be heirs of salvation. The children used to sing in Sunday-school: "I want to be an angel," but in Jesus Christ the believer is lifted to a higher rank than angels, for,

"Never did angels taste, above,
Redeeming grace and dying love."

The humblest believer can preach better than Gabriel could, for he can say, "I am a sinner saved by grace," which no angel can say. And, in the mystical unfoldings of truth in the Apocalyptic visions, whenever saints and angels are seen together, the saints are next the throne, and the angels are round about the saints. Not an angel in all that vast host can say that he belongs to Christ as a member of His body; or in the same sense with the believer, "I am a son of God, and a joint heir with Jesus Christ." Some angels might envy saints, and gladly change places with God's redeemed ones. This is overwhelming, and when it first bursts on the view of a believer, he can hardly restrain himself. He feels as though he had suddenly been lifted up to the highest heaven, and was looking on scenes and hearing sounds which it is "unlawful for a man to utter."

In an American city, a lawyer, much esteemed and high in social life, found in the northern part of the State, among the Indian tribes, a young Indian maiden, in whom he became deeply interested, and whom he ultimately married. He brought her to the city, totally undisciplined and uneducated, though virtuous and ingenuous. He then secured educational culture for her through teachers in English, drawing and music, and gave her such opportunities as wealth and love could afford. Meanwhile, however, she was accepted in society as the wife of a distinguished citizen.

Our Lord Jesus Christ came down into this world to redeem and wed as His bride a believing humanity. He did not, however, stay on the level of humanity, but He carried humanity back with Him toward His own level; and the ultimate end of man's redemption will be that "he that overcometh shall sit with Him on His throne, as He also overcame, and is set down with His Father upon His throne."

No man would dare to say that, were it not written in the Holy Scripture, (Rev. III: 21.)

Four levels are suggested in these two chapters in Hebrews:

(1.) High up above all others, the divine level.

(2.) Far below it, the angelic level.

(3.) A little below that, the human level.

(4.) And below that, the infernal level, that of the fallen angels.

Man was originally on the human or earthly level. Satan comes from beneath—his own level—overcomes man, takes his sceptre, and drags him down to the infernal level; for in the twenty-fifth chapter of Matthew we are told that the same "fire prepared for the devil and his angels" awaits those whom Christ finally condemns as workers of iniquity.

Jesus Christ, coming down from the highest heavens, passed the angelic to the human level; in a sense, He descended to the infernal, that He might there contest the whole matter with the betrayer of man, and "destroy him who had the power of death," and demolish his empire. But, having taken man's nature and betrothed a believing humanity to Himself, was it not in the necessity of the case that, when He went back to His own level, He should carry back with Him, past the angelic level to the heavenly, the redeemed body of humanity that He had wedded? The man whose story has been told did not go down to the plane of the poverty and ignorance of her he wedded, but rather lifted her to his own plane of wealth, intelligence and social position; and our Lord Jesus Christ knew, when He identified Himself with man, that, in so far as He was wedded to a believing humanity, He would lift that believing humanity beyond the human or angelic plane, into the very atmosphere and presence of God. (Comp. John xvii: 21-26).

The glimpse given us here of this marvellous truth, also hints the reason why that mystery of Christ can never be fully unfolded in the present age, but waits for future unveiling—as we are told in the Epistle to the Ephesians: "That in *the ages to come*, He might show what is the exceeding greatness of His love and grace in His kindness toward us in Christ Jesus."

Believing children of God, however delighting in fellowship with Him, are painfully conscious of so many defects, deficiencies, inconsistencies and sins that it is impossible to realize such a future as before them; but the eternal God, with Whom is no past, present or future, and to Whom all coming realities are equally present facts, looks

past existing imperfections, faults, and whatever
is due to the taint of sin in the nature, and sees the
absolute faultlessness which will be apparent
when Christ presents the believer before the
presence of His glory. In God's eye, every saint
is already perfected in Christ Jesus. We do not
see it, here; angels do not see it now, though they
desire to look into the boundless, unfathomable
depths of infinite grace; and so it remains to be
seen in the ages to come, when corruption shall be
left behind forever, and even the body of this
humiliation shall be changed into the likeness of
the body of His glory. Then, in eternal youth,
in the cloudless atmosphere of an untainted joy,
with a perfected holiness, believers will stand before Him; and then, by the Church, shall be made
known to the principalities and powers in heavenly
places, how stupendous was the problem of redemption, and the divine solution of it.

Such a future lies before every believing child
of God. There may be a cripple, a child of crime,
born of drunken and depraved parents, and in the
very body carrying the terrible penalty of the sins
of generations that preceded; and yet in God's eyes
that poor crippled body is lustrous with transfigured glory. The taint of human heredity is
gone, and only the holy heredity of Christ is left.

The corruption of the human blood is displaced by the cleansing of the blood that purges from sin; and that humble disciple,—bodily, mentally and morally a cripple,—contests with angels beauty of character, likeness to God, and unspeakable bliss. It is incredible, but for God's revelation; it is unmatchable, even as a revelation.

Every man makes his election as to who shall be his representative, the first Adam, or the last Adam. Repentance is turning from the first Adam to the second. And, somewhat as we elect a representative in Parliament or Congress, sending one to be the man of our choice, we may elect whether Adam the first or Adam the second shall stand as our representative, before God. The first Adam represents fall and ruin; the last Adam represents rising and restoration, and we may choose between the two. Repentance gives up and renounces all connection with the first Adam, and faith takes the Second Man as representative, henceforth, to call Him Saviour and Lord. This is translation from the kingdom of darkness into the kingdom of light, and from the power of Satan unto God.

In America many years ago, in Boston, Wendell Phillips, the great anti-slavery agitator, heard Dr. Lyman Beecher preach upon God's creative and redemptive right in man. He was so overwhelmed with this thought of what Jesus Christ had done for a lost race, and the claims of redemption upon himself, that he went straight home, literally fell down on his face on the floor of his bedchamber, and said, "O, my God, I belong to Thee. Take Thou thine own." And from that time forth to the day of his death, he bore testimony that he had never seen a thing to be contrary to the will of God without hating it.

We may add that, to a true student of Holy Scripture, there is neither a question that Jesus Christ is Deity, nor that to Him, as Deity, worship belongs.

The late Dr. Fuller, of Baltimore, was a popular, interesting and evangelical preacher. Being zealous for Christian unity, he preached one morning on the necessity and duty of magnifying things that unite, and minimizing the things that divide, believers. He represented this truth in the light of the heavenly state, showing that it is not worth while in this world to make so much of that of which we shall make so little when we meet fellow believers above. In order to show the absurdity of sectarian divisions, he represented those who belong to various Christian bodies, and who were unduly jealous of their denominational history and tenets, as being in heaven and looking around to find their fellow Christians who belonged to the same particular branch of the Church: Baptists looking for their immersed friends, Methodists for their fellow members of class-meetings, Presbyterians for the zealous defenders of Presbyterian ideas of law and order, and Episcopalians looking for the true Apostolic Succession. At the close of his sermon, a Unitarian friend said: "Dr. Fuller, I am surprised at your lack of charity; you really did not represent any Unitarians at all as being in heaven." Dr. Fuller replied: "If you will come to-night, I will give you a glimpse as to the feelings of a Unitarian there." In the course of his sermon, he imagined a Unitarian as stationed with John on the Island of Patmos, and permitted to look and enter through the open door and see the things which should be hereafter, and he described his emotions. In the first place, he witnessed that scene in the fifth chapter of Revelation, where the Book was in the right hand of Him that sat upon the throne, and no man nor angel dared to touch or even to look upon it. The Lion-Lamb of God, slain for sin, but triumphant as a King, came and took the Book, and then he heard the acclamations of the saints: "Thou art worthy to take the Book, and to unloose the seals thereof, for Thou wast slain, and hast redeemed us to God by Thy blood, out of every kindred, and tongue, and people, and nation, and hast made us unto our God kings and priests; and we shall reign on the earth." And round about that company, he observed countless angels, ascribing to the same slain but risen Lamb, all worship: "Worthy is the Lamb that was slain to receive power, and riches, and wisdom, and strength, and honour, and glory, and blessing." He went along a little further, and saw a great multitude standing on the sea of glass, and they were lifting up their voices in similar acclamations, and ascribing "Salvation unto our God, and unto the Lamb." "Why," he said, "there are no Unitarians in that company."

He went a little further, and saw a white horse, and a Conqueror riding upon him, and upon His vesture, and upon His thigh was the mysterious name written: "King of kings, and Lord of lords," and a countless band of worshippers and warriors followed in his train. He went yet further, and saw the New Jerusalem let down from God out of Heaven, having the glory of God. He saw no temple therein, and found that the reason was that the "Lord God Almighty and the Lamb are the Temple of it." He found no light even of the sun therein, and learned that "The Lord God Almighty and the Lamb are the Light of it." And he found on the throne, as joint Sovereigns, God and the Lamb that was slain. "Why," he said, "There is nobody here that does not worship the Lamb jointly with God Himself. I cannot stay here unless I join this worship." And so he moved among the throng and waved his palm; he struck his harp, and cried out: "Worthy is the Lamb that was slain! Salvation unto the Lamb!"

Dr. Fuller concluded his sermon. His Unitarian neighbour walked up the aisle, shook his hand earnestly with both his own, and said: "Jesus Christ has conquered. Let me bow here, and, like Thomas, say 'My Lord, and my God!'"

CHAPTER XI

THE BIBLE AND GOD'S THOUGHTS

THE Golden Milestone, in the City of Rome, was the point at which the many roads, running from all directions in the Empire, met and converged.

By at least fifty different lines of argument and demonstration, we may approach as a goal the conclusion that the Holy Scriptures are of divine origin. To one of these reference has been made hitherto only incidentally, yet its value might well entitle it to fill the space of an entire volume: namely, the mark of God's mind and heart upon this book.

In the fifty-fifth chapter of the prophecy of Isaiah, 8th to 13th verses, there is a distinct challenge from Almighty God to test His Word by two great criteria:

"For my thoughts are not your thoughts;
Neither are your ways, My ways."

(1.) Are the thoughts contained in this book superhuman thoughts? And are the ways or

methods or plans of working suggested here like
unto man's, or unlike unto man's? That is the
first test.

(2.) What is the moral character and power of
this book? Is it superior to all others in moral
and spiritual teaching? And, especially, is it
superior to all ethical or moral systems as a dynamic force in the transformation of character, and
the regeneration of human society?

We confine ourselves for the present to the first:
"My thoughts are not your thoughts"—that is,
God's conceptions of things are not man's conceptions. The method God uses to express this
is to remind us how high the heavens are above the
earth,—even so high are His ways and thoughts
above those of men. They belong to an infinitely
elevated plane; His thoughts of things and ways of
working are not only unlike men's, but are often
opposite or contrary and contradictory to the
dictates of human wisdom.

In Cudworth's "Intellectual System of the Universe," the bottom thought is that the signs of a
divine mind are impressed upon the universe of
matter. The difference between the Corelli Mar-
bles and the blossoming of stone in the Cathedral
of Milan is the difference between the bed-rock in
the quarry, and the sculptured stone that has been

The Thoughts of God

shapen and polished by the genius of a master-ar-
chitect; the difference between the master painting
and the rude pigments on the palette, is that brains
are mixed with the colours,—the artist's mind
manifests itself on the canvas. If a mass of iron
filings are put upon a sheet of paper and a bar
magnet underneath, there will be a strange activity
on the part of the iron filings: they will assume,
as though instinct with life, various circular and
spiral forms, each particle attaching itself to those
on either side. The invisible current of the
magnet shapes that chaos into the symmetry and
beauty of a cosmos.

The Bible is composed of letters and words and
sentences, but an invisible current of Divine Life
pervades the book, and makes it God's Living
Oracles, and so its contents assume beauty, proportion, symmetry. Letters form into words;
words into sentences, and sentences into para-
graphs in which the mind of God is expressed.
Just so far as it is possible that a book should be,
this book is the mirror of the mind of God. His
intellectual impress is on it, organising its truths
into a divine system, and there is no other book
that compares with it as to the intellectual rank
of its contents.

The word "idea" has been thought by some to

combine two Latin words—*in Deo*—"a thought in God"—a conception that is first in the divine mind. In this sense the Bible is full of *ideas;* thoughts that, born in the mind of God, belong to a far more exalted plane than the thoughts of men.

For instance, the idea of *Infinity*—a word which seems to express the natural or essential attribute of deity, in a general way, better than most others. Infinite literally means "without bounds." There is no limit to God—to His power, for He is omnipotent; to His knowledge for He is omniscient; to His presence, for He is omnipresent; to His existence, for He is eternal. He is not only infinite, but immutable, without change as without bounds, for change implies either degeneracy or improvement—a change for worse or for better; but God, being perfect, cannot change; infinity therefore involves immutability.

Such an idea of infinity, with its necessary correlative, immutability, is a conception of God drawn from his Word and found nowhere else. The story is that when Mr. Gillespie was called upon, in that great Westminster assembly, to pray—the assembly at the time seeking some proper designation or definition of God—he began: "O, God, Thou art a Spirit, Infinite, Eternal and Unchangeable in Thy Being, Wisdom, Power, Holiness,

The Thoughts of God

Justice, Goodness and Truth;" and there came upon that body at once the conviction that God had given a definition of Himself, in the opening sentence of that prayer; and so those very words came to be embodied in that compendium of doctrine, "the Westminster Catechism."

Where did Gillespie get this conception? Not from any heathen source or human writing, but from a long, reverent and prayerful study of the Word of God. There alone he learned that God is a Spirit, Infinite, Eternal, Unchangeable.

The Grand Cañon of the Colorado, in America, is one of the wonders of the world. It is an immense chasm, twelve miles in width, and two hundred miles in length, with perpendicular walls six thousand feet high on each side. Sixty cities like the metropolis of the world with all its hundred suburbs could be put in that chasm; the Falls of Niagara or the Falls of Victoria, in some of the fissures of those rocks, would seem no more than a mountain cascade. St. Paul's Cathedral at London or St. Peter's at Rome would be a mere child's toy on the floor of that great chasm; but even this gives no adequate conception of God's infinity.

Sirius, the brightest of the fixed stars, is so far off that its light, flying 186,000 miles a second, took nearly nine years to get to this planet. There are other stars, within the reach of telescopic vision whose rays took twenty, forty, eighty, a hundred years to reach us. The interstellar spaces are so vast that our entire solar system, dropped in the sea of this immeasurable infinitude, would be but as a few pebbles dropped in the ocean. He who hewed out the Grand Cañon of the Colorado, who stretched out the interstellar spaces of the heavens, is the God that gave this Book, and it shows that He is its Author, for in it we constantly meet the thoughts and terms of infinity, the natural dialect of God.

We have already seen, when adverting to the vast distances and dimensions of space, what language the Word of God uses. "As the heavens are higher than the earth"—not the heavens where the clouds float, a few miles up; not the heavens where the visible stars are seen, though millions upon millions of miles away; but the depths that no telescope can penetrate, beyond even the power of photography though it catches the image of stars invisible even to the telescopic eye. That is the way God speaks in the Bible. No one else would naturally use such terms, or knows enough to do so. They befit Almighty God only.

Again, "As the heaven is high above the earth,

The Thoughts of God

so great is His mercy toward them that fear Him. As far as the East is from the West, so far hath He removed our transgressions from us.... The mercy of the Lord is from everlasting to everlasting upon them that fear Him."* Here are the three dimensions of astronomy: Infinite height, breadth, and length. Go as high as we may, there is still a height beyond. However far we go east, there is still an east; however far west, there is a west beyond. God says of sins forgiven, that they are banished to such remoteness that only infinite opposite directions can express it. "And from everlasting to everlasting"—from an eternity that had no beginning to an eternity that has no end—that is the way He measures the length or duration of His love. Four dimensions are similarly united in the third chapter of the Epistle to the Ephesians: "That ye may know the breadth"—which is universal comprehension and infinite mercy; "and the length," which is eternity; "and the depth," going down to hell to pluck us out; "and the height," going up to the throne of God to carry us there. The Infinite God is the Author of this Bible: "His thoughts are not man's thoughts, neither are man's ways His ways," and it is written as though God wrote it; it is consistent

* Psalm CIII.

with its claims of Authorship; it has His marks upon it.

Take the Biblical conception of God as a Being—the divine nature. God is represented in the Holy Scripture as Trinity—not three Gods, nor an association or combination of three in one; but a Trinity, implying three persons, but one nature.

Three definitions God gives of Himself: "The Fountain of Life," "Light," "Love." These three words are the keys to the Gospel according to John; and the first Epistle of John; and by these three words, their secret chambers are unlocked. Life stands for the sum of all being; Light, for the sum of all intellectual excellence; and Love, for the sum of all moral excellence. Hence God is Life, Light and Love; for, if He be the sum of all being, of all intellectual and of all moral excellence, nothing remains to be predicted of Him; everything else is already included.

God told Moses, when he asked his name, that he might answer the Children of Israel when they should ask, "Who is He that sent you?" "I am that I am," i. e., "I am He Who am forever." Afterward He compressed it into two words: "I AM—hath sent you."* "I am"—the present tense of the verb "to be," joined with the first

* Exodus IV.

216

The Thoughts of God

personal pronoun, expresses not only the idea of endless existence, but of an eternal *present*. This is another divine conception, found nowhere else but in the Bible. Jesus Christ uses similar language when He says to the Jews, "Before Abraham was I–AM"—not "I was."* Abraham had a past, present and future, but Jesus, being equal with the Father, has the past and future equally present before Him, and His existence is one eternal Now, without the successions of time that pertain to our moral existence. The thoughts of God are not as man's thoughts.

According to the Bible conception, man has a three-fold nature: "I pray God your whole *spirit*, and *soul* and *body* be preserved blameless unto the coming of our Lord Jesus Christ.† This idea recurs in other Scriptures (I Cor. ii, and Heb. iv : 12) where the distinction between soul and spirit is brought out. The soul is the natural man, that does not see or know the things of God, and the spirit is the highest part of the man, capable of direct communication with God, enlightened and illumined by the Holy Spirit. "The dividing asunder of soul and spirit," hints at a realm between the two, which, though connected with each, pertains exclusively to neither, and in which

* John viii.   † I Thess. v : 23.

middle realm of being, the "thoughts and intents of the heart" are generated.

Such passages of Scripture, which, together with others, unfold the Bible doctrine of man's three-fold nature, suggest a three-storied house, the upper story, an observatory, with skylights and majestic windows that look out on celestial prospects; the body, the lowest story, with its five senses,—sight, hearing, taste, touch and smell, opening out into the external universe, like doors and windows, through which to gather information about things without, and report to the soul, which is like the second story of the building, shut in and in darkness, but getting by way of the body, through the avenues of the senses, knowledge with regard to the external world. The topmost story, the spirit, the highest of all, is alone capable of direct knowledge of God, and an intimate communion and fellowship with Him. The soul seems to be that part of man's complex being which may thus derive its information with regard to the world without, through the senses; or of higher truth, through the intuitions of the spirit, which gets its knowledge not through the body or soul only, but through intuition and direct revelation from God. And, in the mysterious realm lying between the two, imagination, mem-

ory, conscience, sensibility, reason, will, gather
impulses through body, soul and spirit, and so
moral judgments and decisions are formed.

Hence the disaster of the fall. When man fell,
the spirit became a death chamber—the windows,
darkened, the skylights covered, shut in; nothing
left but intuitions, and those not by any means
infallible; the vision of heaven and the stars
lost. Regeneration is the kindling anew, in
that spiritual death-chamber, of the life of God.
The Tabernacle may beautifully represent the
same truth,—the outer court, the body; the holy
place within the veil, the soul; the holiest place
within the second veil, the spirit. And, when man
sinned, the Shekinah fire was quenched, but,
when God in Jesus Christ, gives the Spirit back
to man in regeneration, the Shekinah fire glows
again, and fills that inner place with divine light.
Such conceptions of man are peculiar to the Bible.
They are the thoughts of God about man.

The story of the creation of woman, whether
treated as history, poem, or parable, is one of the
most beautiful conceptions in Holy Scripture.
God made a deep sleep to fall upon Adam, opened
his side and took out one of the ribs, and made it
into a woman, and brought her to the man, and He
said to the man, "Bone of thy bone; flesh of thy

flesh; thy counterpart." The word means not helpmeet, but "one over against him," as bone corresponds to socket, as mortice to tenon; a counterpart, one apposite to him, not opposite. Each was adapted to the other so that the proficiencies of the one make up for the deficiencies of the other, and contrariwise. Eve was taken out of Adam's side; as some one has suggested, not out of his head to rule over him; nor out of his arm to be his tool; nor out of his foot to be his slave; but out of his breast, nearest his heart, to be nourished, cherished, loved; his equal, his companion, his counterpart. But it took God to think such a thought, and write such a record. It is like Him to have done things that way.

The Bible conception of two worlds is grand— the universe, partly seen, partly unseen; partly temporal and transitory, passing away, taking different shapes and forms, waste going on and replenishment; partly unseen, invisible, eternal, immutable. Life is a ladder. Like any ladder, it rests on things below, and reaches to things above; and, as you go up, you leave things, below, farther down and approach nearer to things at the top. Life's ladder rests on material things that may be tested by the five senses; we mount one rung, and meet what can be tested only by four senses out of the five; another rung, and we meet what can be tested by only three; then by two; still another rung, and we find what can be tested only by one, like light, which appeals to the eye, but not to the hearing, touch, taste, or smell, yet it belongs to the material realm. Still higher, we come to verities that pertain to the universe and have to do with matter, yet which no sense ever has discerned. Life was never seen, heard, touched, tasted, or smelt. Yet, do you doubt it? What makes the difference between a living body and a corpse? The corpse has the same features, eyes and ears, hands and feet; but there is something in a living body that is not in a corpse. Put a living human being in a metallic casket and seal it up air-tight. You have scarce done it before something has fled which you cannot keep in with walls nor keep out by locked doors. Nobody knows what it is, but it is real. What the Bible teaches is that, as we go from this lower sphere up this ladder of life, we come to an unseen and invisible realm, far greater, grander, more important than what the senses perceive; and that God has given us other senses by which to explore this invisible realm. In the fifth chapter of the Epistle to the Hebrews, we read of the "senses exercised to discern good and evil"—not physical senses, of course, which cannot discern good and evil, but another set of senses which are to be exercised upon intellectual and moral subjects. Faith is the sense of the invisible; hope is the sense of the future; memory is the sense of the past; sensibility is the sense of moral attraction and repulsion. Such are some of the senses God has given to explore the invisible world.

Many other divine thoughts are found in this Book, and nowhere else. God's thoughts are not man's; they are above and often, also, contradictory to the ideas of man.

What is man's notion of love? His love is guided by his liking. He loves what he thinks is lovable, and where advantage is to be got from loving, in the response of reciprocal affection. Man gives where he can get. How different God's love. He loves without reference to His likings, or He would never have loved sinners. He loves what is unlovable that He may make it lovable. He gives lavishly and infinitely, and gives the best He has to those from whom He receives nothing. Such is the difference between God's ways and man's ways. Man loves and gives for the sake of being loved and receiving gifts; God loves where He is not loved and never will be, and gives where He does not, and never will, receive.

What is God's idea of greatness? "The kings of

the nations exercise lordship over them, and they that are great exercise authority upon them; but it shall not be so among you (Matt. xx: 25. Luke xxii: 25.) . . ." Jesus, taking off His outer garments, and putting on the slave's apron, and girding Himself, took a basin of water and washed the disciples' feet, wiping them with the towel wherewith He was girded. The two most menial offices that could be performed by a Jew, were to unlatch the shoe and to wash the feet. Christ did not unlatch the shoes, because they had been left in the vestibule as the disciples had come into the banqueting room; the only other menial act He could do, to descend to the lowest depths of drudgery, was to wash their feet. The Creator of all worlds and creatures, washed the feet of His own disciples. Is there anything like that outside the Bible?

Take the idea of incarnation. God, made flesh, and coming to dwell among men, does not take His place where He belongs, at the top of the social pyramid, but at the bottom. He associates Himself with the poorest and lowest and least of earth. Christ never owned a square foot of territory on the world He made. He was the object of charity, even the clothes He wore no doubt being the gift of women that ministered to Him of their substance. He had nothing, yet He owned everything. What conceptions these are! And when Christ died for man, it was not after a respectable, not to say, honorable fashion, like a general, falling in battle. The Creator and Redeemer of mankind was crucified between thieves, having been first exchanged for a robber and murderer. Such is the unique and paradoxical character of God's ideas and ways.

How, again, infinite simplicity of method is combined with infinite sublimity of teaching. Take God's account of creation: "In the beginning God created the heaven and the earth." Then put alongside it Mr. Herbert Spencer's final definition of evolution:

"Evolution is an integration of matter and concomitant dissipation of motion; during which the matter passes from an indefinite, incoherent homogeneity to a definite, coherent heterogeneity; and during which the retained motion undergoes a parallel transformation."

Suppose the Bible were written in that style. Even the metaphysicians themselves could not understand it. What kind of a book would that be to put into the hands of little children to learn the way of life? "Heterogeneity," "homogeneity" and "parallel transformation!" God is divinely simple. "To as many as received Him, to them gave He power to become the sons of God, even to them that believe on His name." Believing, then, is *receiving*—the simplest act of which we are capable. "God so loved the world, that He gave His only begotten Son, that whosoever believeth in Him should not perish, but have everlasting life." If God *gave*, all man has to do is to *take*. There are seven words in the Bible used to express this initial act of faith, and they all convey one idea—reception: Look, hear, taste, take, come, trust, choose. To take in a prospect, we look; to take in music, we hear; to take in food, we taste; to receive a gift, we take; to take in a territory, we come, or walk; to take a friend, we trust; to take a resolve, we choose. So easy to be understood, that the simplest can grasp all that is necessary. Not only God's infinity, sublimity, and divine originality, but His simplicity, are impressed on the Scriptures indelibly.

These are Living Oracles. His vitality is inbreathed into this Book, and man cannot destroy it. A colossal statue of "Liberty" stands in New York Harbour, and every night the birds, dashing against the lantern, beat themselves into insensibility, and fall at its base; and, in the morning, heaps of carcasses are found there, dead. But the light shines on, quenchless, serene. Satan's birds of the night beat against God's light, threatening to put it out and leave the world in darkness, but they are like waves that beat against the rocks only to cleave themselves in twain. As well attempt to put out the stars or the sun with a watering pot. When all those who oppose and assault the Word of God have gone into the darkness of perpetual night, that Light will still shine on, and many a poor mariner will by it be guided to the harbour of everlasting rest.

CHAPTER XII

The Bible and God's Ethics

A lofty mountain-peak commands a whole horizon, but the human vision can take in but a part of that horizon circle, at one view. Hence, a new outlook and in a new direction is possible from the same commanding point of prospect. Again we recur to that leading utterance in the Prophecy of Isaiah:

"My thoughts are not your thoughts, neither are your ways My ways," saith the Lord. "For as the heavens are high above the earth, so are My ways higher than your ways, and My thoughts higher than your thoughts. For as the rain cometh down, and the snow from heaven, and returneth not thither, but watereth the earth, and maketh it bring forth and bud, that it may give seed to the sower, and bread to the eater; so shall My word be that goeth forth out of My mouth: it shall not return unto Me void; but it shall accomplish that which I please, and it shall prosper in the thing whereto I sent it." And in the last verse: "Instead of the thorn, shall come up the fir tree, and instead of the brier shall come up the myrtle tree; and it (that is, this transformation of the soil of society and of the human heart) shall be to the Lord for a name (that is, a 'fame' or 'reputation') for an everlasting sign that shall not be cut off."

We have already seen, how, from the intellectual side, the Bible reveals God's thoughts, as infinitely above man's conceptions, and His ways of working contrary to as well as superior to man's methods.

In the moral aspect of the Bible, also, God's conceptions are infinitely above man's ethics, and His moral and spiritual ways of working are utterly beyond man's philosophy. The Bible has proved also the great moral dynamic, the one divinely potent force for the regeneration of human beings and the transformation of human society.

This Scripture affirms, what is very striking, a complete moral revolution through God's Word. "Thorn and thistles" were the original marks of the curse: "Thorns and thistles shall the earth bring forth unto thee," was the sign of man's fall, which was to be seen and shown in the very ground on which he trod. There is an obvious reference to this here. Instead of these signs of the curse, there shall be tokens of blessings. Instead of thorns and thistles, which are vexatious, harmful,

noxious, shall come up the fir tree—an evergreen—
the myrtle, graceful and fragrant—a refreshing
shade tree and a beautiful ornament to the garden.
That is to say, what is hurtful, offensive, destructive, shall be displaced by what is beautiful, fruitful, helpful. This moral miracle is to stand in all
history for the establishment of God's reputation
as a God that doeth wonders; and, whatever other
signs may not continue, this shall be His everlasting sign. The deaf may no longer hear, the blind
no longer see, the lepers no longer be cleansed,
and the dead be no longer raised up, as in the time
of Christ. These miracles may have had some
special mission in the authenticating of Christ's
claims, at the beginning; but, whatever other
miracles are not continuous and continual, this
moral miracle, God says, shall not be cut off. As
long as the Word of God is preached, these moral
and spiritual transformations shall attend and
follow to the end of time.

We look first at some of the moral features of
the Oracles of God; and, then, ascending to the
higher level, consider some of its spiritual features,
which belong to a more exalted realm.

That which most closely touches morality, is
Law, and we, therefore, glance first at God's system
of legislation as laid down in the Book, brevity

compelling only a hint here and there, skirting the borders of the subject.

The Ten Words, known as the Decalogue, summarize God's moral law: "God spake all these words." There is singular completeness in the moral law: Two tables, four commandments being assigned to the first, six commandments to the second. And the order as well as the completeness is very noticeable.

(1.) Thou shalt have no other gods before me." No other deity to be tolerated in the presence of Jehovah, Who is to stand absolutely alone,—no competitor or rival, no division of interest or worship.

(2.) "Thou shalt not make unto thee any graven image." God is not to be worshipped by the aid of visible representations, whether furnished by the art of the painter or of the sculptor and graver. The Bible is firmly set against all visible impersonations or representations of Deity, and we ought to understand that fact, for this command is violated even in thousands of Christian homes, and so-called Christian Churches. These pictures and images of God are all contrary to the second commandment, because, whenever He is represented thus, the tendency is for the imagination to stop with the image, so that, instead of worshipping the Living

The Ethics of God

God, man pays homage to a material human representation. There is a further danger,—for this leads directly to grosser forms of idolatry. The worship of the golden calf was not meant as idolatry; the calf was set up as a representation of Jehovah.* The gods afterward brought in from Tyre and Sidon and Phœnicia,—Baal and Astarte, were foreign deities—idols proper. But the former prepared the way for the latter, and it is always so.

(3.) "Thou shalt not take the name of the Lord thy God in vain,"—even the name of God to be held in holy reverence, and not spoken needlessly, vainly, carelessly, for His name represents His nature—Himself.

(4.) "Remember the Sabbath Day to keep it holy"—Setting a fence of restriction around sacred time, that man may have a chance to look away from objects near by to the far horizons, from what is temporal to what is eternal, and from things human to things divine. Some would try to make it appear that the Sabbath was a Mosaic institution and has no longer any obligation; but the weekly day of rest is one of two things that were ordained in, and have come down from, a sinless Eden. The Sabbath was before Moses, before Adam; and the only other relic of the

* Exodus xxxii: 5-8.

231

primitive Paradise is marriage—ideal marriage. As well make marriage a matter of Mosaic legislation as the Sabbath law, since both of them were thus instituted and ordained for man in Eden, before the fall.

The second great table of the Law enjoins six duties:

(5.) "Honour thy father and thy mother . . ." There is a period in human life when the only God the child knows is the father and mother: not being able yet to grasp the idea of Deity, the parent stands between the child and the conception of God, and, if the child learns to honour and obey the father and mother, afterward, when the conception of Deity dawns on the understanding, it is comparatively easy to transfer filial obedience and love from the human parent to the divine, from the father on earth to the Father in Heaven. One reason why there is so little piety, even in co-called Christian families, is because parental discipline and childlike obedience are so rare. Children are not only outgrowing all obedience to parental authority, but many of them never knew what it was, and could not outgrow it. A most shameful state of things is this; and it saps the foundations of all human wellbeing. If there is no obedience in the family, there will be no true obedience in the

The Ethics of God

State or Church. Lawlessness in all human society naturally follows lawlessness in the household.

The commandments of the second table follow a descending series from the most necessary and important to those of subordinate character; or from the general to the specific.

(6.) "Thou shalt not kill." Life is the first interest to be guarded, because, if life is not protected, nothing else can be.

(7.) "Thou shalt not commit adultery." Next to life is family purity, else how shall the child know even who is his own father? *"Ipso facto"* the marriage relation is dissolved by marital infidelity, and such infidelity is just as ruinous, and just as desecrating on the part of the man as on the part of the woman. Away with these lax notions that wink at sin in the man, and condemn it in the woman!

(8.) "Thou shalt not steal." Next to the guards put about life and marital purity are those about property.

(9.) "Thou shalt not bear false witness against thy neighbour." His reputation is also to be guarded as one of his most sacred possessions. Shakespeare sagaciously inveighs against robbing one of his "good name."

(10.) "Thou shalt not covet," or "Thou shalt not lust." Lust covers all irregular, all abnormal desires. At the end of the commandments, at last we get down to that which constitutes the root of all crime—unholy, inordinate desire.

What a moral compendium of duty, and all the ten, reducible to two! The first of all commandments is "Thou shalt love the Lord thy God with all thy heart, and soul, and mind, and strength. And the second is like unto it, Thou shalt love thy neighbour as thyself. Upon these two commandments hang all the law and the prophets," is our Lord's own commentary; and even the two are further reducible to one. "Love worketh no ill" to God or man, and therefore, "love is the fulfilling of the law." There is no other moral code like that. Individual hints may be found similar to it, but the morality of the Bible is an indigenous plant, in its own soil—not an exotic, out of its native atmosphere and surroundings.

The moral law implies moral administration, and so the Word of God teaches the doctrine of God's Providence, which is set forth, once for all, in the Book of Esther. All the great principles of God's Providence are laid down in this book, such as these:

The Ethics of God

(1.) There is a hand behind human affairs that shapes and moulds them.

(2.) That hand forbears for the time being, so that adversity sometimes comes to the good, and prosperity to the wicked.

(3.) That hand distributes th e ultimate awards of virtue and righteousness in happiness, and the ultimate awards of wickedness and vice in misery.

(4.) That hand weaves the smallest incidental matters into the fabric of Divine Purpose,—such as the sleeplessness of the king, and the unwillingness of Mordecai to pay homage to Haman.

(5.) That hand administers poetic retribution, so associated with and correspondent with sin, that there is no mistaking the hand of the God of Recompenses—witness Haman's death on the very scaffold he had prepared for Mordecai.

(6.) God's hand does not compel human action. Providence is not fatali m. God ordains, but He does not violate human freedom, which is among the things decreed. When Esther went into the presence of Ahasuerus, it was by her own choice and on her own responsibility; she went praying, and with the support of her own maidens. It was her own act, yet according to God's decree.

(7.) Last of all, the hand that guides affairs is a hidden hand—does not appear visibly, manifestly;

the effects are seen, but not the cause. Hence, while the name of God is not found in Esther, the workings of Almighty God are there, not only seen by faith, but may be found even by the ungodly. No other teaching on Providence is necessary after this one book is mastered, for no new additional principle in the divine philosophy of administration is introduced afterward.

The Bible teaches also a Final Judgment—an ultimate adjudication of affairs of government. The adjustment of sin and penalty is not always complete in this world, for the scales of divine judgment do not hang evenly, this side of the veil; only beyond are they seen to be in perfect equilibrium.

It is a sublime conception of judgment which the Bible contains:

He is a God of—

(1.) Infinite knowledge, so that nothing can be hid from His eye.

(2.) Infinite power, so that nothing can escape His pursuit.

(3.) Omnipresence, so that there is no part of the universe where His knowledge and power do not penetrate.

(4.) Infinite justice, so that He cannot be bribed,

or blinded; nor can any influence pervert or prevent His judgments.

(5.) Yet, after all, His wrath is as holy as all else about Him. Many do not like to talk about God's wrath; they avoid it as though it were a kind of blotch on the divine character. The wrath of God is just as much a perfection as His love, for there is nothing that is not perfect in Him. Wrath in God is not man's passion elevated to a divine sphere and level. This is a total misconception. Wrath in God is not a passion at all; it is rather a principle. It is not variable, capricious, changeable; it is eternal, and immutable, like everything else in Him.

When a magnetic needle is set on its pivot it swings toward the pole. If approached at one end with another magnet, it attracts; approached at the other, it repels; by the same law it attracts at one end and repels at the other. So the same attribute of divine benevolence attracts holiness at one pole, and repels wickedness at the other— the same perfection in both cases, with two opposite manifestations. This is the God of the Bible— an infinitely perfect God.

God's method of reformation is totally different from man's. Man, whenever he sees an evil, strikes at it; but when God sees an evil, He does not always strike at that particular form of wrong-doing: He puts a lever underneath the whole character, and elevates its whole level, because to suppress one form of evil is to give a chance for another to break out in some other form elsewhere. Social evils abounded in the time of Jesus Christ— polygamy, unchastity, infanticide, capricious divorce, bloody and brutal games; wars, rapacious and cruel; death and punishment by torture, caste and slavery. Our Lord mentions and deals specifically with but one of these, and that was capricious divorce. Yet His teaching puts beneath all things evil that pertain to society, a lever greater than that of which Archimedes dreamed, and overturns them all.

Again, human reformers begin with the outside, and try to work toward the inside, but do not often succeed. God begins with the inside, and lets the outside take care of itself, beginning not with the reformation of external character, but the regeneration of the heart. "Out of the abundance of the heart the mouth speaketh," and out of the heart "flow the issues of life." Hence, God's method of reformation.

Notice also God's idea of character. There is a kind of moral spectrum, similar to the solar spectrum with its colours. There are seven virtues inculcated in the Bible, which, together, comprise this whole spectrum of moral character.

First of all, truth, because truth is the basis of all the rest.   There can be no high, noble character if there be no truth.   Sincerity is at the bottom of all pure and true development.

Faith, hope, love—the peculiar trinity of graces referred to in I Cor. XIII.

Humility, the unconscious grace.   They who think themselves humble, never are.   This takes the form of reverence, also, which is the very soul of worship.

Patience, the enduring grace, which gives permanence to all the rest.

Mercy, like unto God in the peculiar scope and nobility of its forgiveness.   How complete this category!

Truth leads all the rest.   The Bible is in eternal antagonism to anything of the nature of pretension and hypocrisy.   It knows nothing of "policy," and gives no countenance whatever to compromise. What is right, is to be done; what is wrong, to be let alone.

In "Jane Eyre," Charlotte Bronte gives a very fine touch of satire.   She makes Mr. Brocklehurst to say: "I have a little boy, younger than you, who knows six Psalms by heart; and when you ask him which he would rather have, a gingerbread nut to eat, or a verse of a Psalm to learn, he says: 'Oh, the the verse of a Psalm.' 'Angels sing Psalms,' says he; 'I wish to be a little angel here below;' He then gets two nuts in recompense of his infant piety." This boy found Psalm liking better policy than cake liking, for appetite got but one gingerbread nut, and piety got two. Thus the author ran her stiletto through the fair exterior of thousands of lives that are regulated by nothing but policy, and are very pious, not on principle, but for the sake of the gingerbread nuts. But the Bible knows no such ethical farce. It is the most transparent book in its moral teaching that was ever given to the human race, and it teaches men to be transparent. That Greek word for "sincerity" means what can bear the searching exposure of the sun's rays, what can stand being held up to view, disclosing its innermost self.

What is the Bible idea of humility, for which the Greek language offered no proper word? the only one available, expressing fawning servility, as of one who, in bondage to a tyrannical master, gets down and licks his feet. Many people confound humility with humiliation, which is different.

The Ethics of God

Humiliation is conscious; humility, unconscious.*

Love is the crowning grace. When faith is lost in sight, and hope in fruition, love will be the reigning spirit about the throne of God—the ethical force of gravitation in God's moral universe. What is love? It is the divine principle of life, the royal law, of preferring somebody else to one's self, self-giving for the sake of others. Love, therefore, surrenders self to God with supreme preference for Him; and surrenders self to man—yielding one's own interests in order to promote that of others. Love is, therefore, the law of life that gives self to God, first of all, and, secondarily, to man.

Such a law of love allows no room for a trace of resentment. A story is told of General Robert E. Lee, that when at West Point there was a rival for honours, who hated Lee because he was his superior in scholarship. Years after, when both were in political life, Lee was asked his opinion of his former rival as a candidate for a certain post. He said: "He is a man of fine qualities and large acquisitions; I think he will adorn the position." "Evidently you do not know what he has been

* One of Dr. Lyman Beecher's sons, entering the ministry, preached for his father. He tried to make a splurge and succeeded. On his way home he said: "That was a very poor effort; I am much humbled, father." "Fudge," he said, "you are only humiliated."

saying against you," was the rejoinder. He quietly answered: "I was asked, not what is his opinion of me, but what is my opinion of him." Such magnanimity is seldom known except by those who have been touched with the transforming power of the divine Spirit of love. Love that worketh no ill to one's neighbor, harbours no ill will even to one's enemy.

The Bible furnishes a divinely perfect ethical standard. It is common to say, in apology for the lax doctrine and notions of biblical inspiration, now permeating even the churches, that the Bible is not needed as an infallible guide, because man has reason and conscience. But there is the more reason why we need the Bible as a final arbiter in ethics. A watch may keep good time, but needs to be corrected by the chronometer, and even the chronometer by the Pole star, for "underneath the stars nothing goes exactly right." Conscience and reason are like watches, and even the *communis consensus* of believers is at best only like the chronometer; but he who would be absolutely certain must look up higher, to God's Polar Star. God gives us in his Word an infallible standard, correct, accurate, trustworthy; to give up its infallibility is, in a sense, to surrender the Bible altogether as an ultimate standard; and no celestial pole star is left us to correct the variations of the moral magnetic needle!

Spiritual things belong to even a higher plane than the moral. The Bible conception of the holiness of God may be taken as an example. "Thou art of purer eyes than to behold evil, and canst not look on iniquity." (Habakkuk 1:13). What a conception of a character, absolutely immaculate, impeccable. "God cannot be tempted with evil," (James 1:13). The word used here is a striking word. It means that, as touching evil, God is "simple," as we say of an innocent little child—too simple to do evil. He has no experimental conception of evil, which perhaps was impossible to the divine nature, practically, before the incarnation, but we know little about such mysteries as these.

We have already referred to love as a law and its general meaning; but love, as it is found in perfection in God, is beyond man's conception. Ruskin writes of pools, outside of manufacturing towns, where muddy water, sand, clay and soot are all mixed together. Let the sun have time and what will it do? It will take out the clay and make of it a sapphire; it will turn the sand into an opal; the soot into a diamond; and the water into crystal snowflakes. God's love shines on the filthy pool of the human heart, and, if it responds to His shining, that love will change the pool into a paradise —transforming the very nature of the man. This love of God is the moral miracle, the wonder of the ages. This is the dynamic force that transforms character and conduct into His own likeness. What manner of man it makes! Men that have holiness like unto God, a new and divine nature by a new birth from above. God coming down and taking up man into Himself; somewhat as in nature, the upper kingdoms reach down and take up what belongs to the lower into themselves—as the vegetable takes up the mineral, and the animal, the vegetable. So God's love reaches down from heaven to take man up into Himself, and give him His own new nature, with its new affinities.

Rev. J. H. Jowett says, "Whenever man tries to make a social classification, it is perpendicular—lower, middle, and upper strata, with half a dozen intermediate layers. When God makes a classification, it is horizontal, right and left: 'He that is not with Me, is against Me.' " It is either yea or nay; good or bad; and differences in the degrees of unholiness and sinfulness look to God, at His distance, and with His perfection, more insignificant than the differences in elevation on the surface of the earth would look at the distance of the sun.

The Ethics of God

God's classification is into sinners and saints; wicked or righteous; friends of God, or foes of God; and there is no intermediate ground. No man can 'stand on the fence' in his relation to Him: he is with the devil or with Jesus Christ. It is a delusive idea that there is any negative or neutral ground, in the universe, as to moral and spiritual questions and issues.

A new relation is disclosed in the Bible between obedience, faith and knowledge. In the scientific sphere, and in the natural world, men believe what they know and understand; in the spiritual world, men know and understand what they believe. In the scientific and natural world, men obey no further than they understand; in the spiritual world, men understand no further than they obey: "If any man will do His will, he shall know of the doctrine." God as a teacher follows His own unique methods. The pupils in his school are never sure of a second lesson till they have learned and practiced the first. Men may go through a college, and come out, knowing scarce more than when they went in; but on God's ladder it is only by stepping on one rung that one is able to ascend to the next, and so, by putting into practice each lesson taught, rise higher in the knowledge and revelation of God. "His ways are not men's ways."

The grand sevenfold consummation of all the Redemption plan is given in the twenty-second chapter of Revelation:

"And there shall be no more curse."—Perfect sinlessness.

"And the throne of God and of the Lamb shall be in it."—Perfect authority.

"And His servants shall serve Him."—Perfect obedience.

"And they shall see His face."—Perfect communion.

"And His name shall be in their foreheads."—Perfect consecration.

"And there shall be no night there."—Perfect blessedness.

"And they shall reign forever and ever."—Perfect glory.

What visions of such sevenfold perfection are found any where outside of the Oracles of God!

This is a favorable point for indicating some practical thoughts and final conclusions.

(1.) Ruskin finely hints in his "Open Sesame," that it is the privilege of a reader to enter into the inmost thought of an author. Hence the democracy of the printed page. If one would get access to the great and notable of earth, he will find a thousand difficulties and obstacles between him and them,—distance, seclusion, locked doors, other engagements—hindrances, purposely put in the way; but whosoever wants to hold communion with God, finds in his Word an open door. He may enter into the secret chambers of God if he searches His Word: "The meek will He guide in judgment; and the meek will He teach His way;" "He will show them the secrets of His covenant." This Book opens the door into the very presence chamber of God and secures audience with Him; and those who reverently approach, and who are willing to bow low enough to enter the low doorway, will find themselves in the palace of the King.

(2.) The greatest sign of the quality of any book is the residuum it leaves behind, as it flows through the mind. As in streams where sulphur abounds, the green deposit is on the stones; and where iron abounds, the red hue is in the bed; and where gold is found, its lustre is on the very sand; so when a book flows through the mind, the supreme testimony to its quality is what it leaves behind. Is it vice or virtue; is it magnanimity, or pusilanimity; is it carnality or spirituality? The greatest proof, perhaps, that the Bible is the Book of God is that it leaves as residuum the gold of heaven, where it flows.

Here is a challenge to all infidels. One of the greatest mysteries in this world is this Book, like which there is nothing else. How did that Book come to be? The wisest cannot possibly account for it. There is nothing else like it on the earth; it is evidently a foreign product. No philosophy has ever accounted for it except by its own account of itself. But it is a fact, which, if human philosophy cannot account for it, even human philosophy must admit to be a fact—and the great dynamic force of the moral universe.

When the mutineers of the *Bounty* landed on Pitcairn Island they had only two books in their possession, one a prayer book and the other a Bible; and there was not a converted man or woman among them. Adams, the leader, read that Bible, found Christ in it, became a transformed man, and, with that as the entire statute book of his little colony, that community became likewise transformed.

When Johnson went down to Sierra Leone in 1816, he found a promiscuous lot of savages, taken out of the holds of slave ships, and put there as on a sort of dumping ground for thieves and robbers and social refuse. Within seven years, the native converts had put up a stone church that would hold a thousand; their children were in Christian schools; they themselves were gathered in Christian congregations, and not a relic of the former orgies and revels of their licentious heathen life remained.

A most godly man recently died in London, of a most painful disease. The surgeon that waited upon him was an infidel when he first went into his bedroom. A little while before the death of this patient a friend said to him: "I wish you had the faith of that man in your heart!" Said he, "I have. I was an infidel once, but I could not remain an infidel in the presence of that deathbed."

A well-known English clergyman had a daughter of sixteen, gay, giddy, thoughtless. She was brought to Jesus Christ, and from that moment the Word of God became the food of her heart, and she could not be restrained from Bible study. One day she said: "Father, won't you read with me?" They turned to the Bible, the one book she wanted, and opened at the twenty-second chapter of Revelation. They read alternately, till they came to the verse, "And they shall see His face," and she suddenly departed to see His face.

The Bible is thus perpetually proving itself the great dynamic. There is no other like it, and when infidels will show us any other book that compares with it in moral and spiritual conceptions, and dynamic power, it will be time enough to swerve from allegiance to it, and consider whether it is worth while to give it up; but, till then, let us stand by The Oracles of God.

(3.) The conclusion forces itself upon us that this is the first among all books, viewed from whatever side, whether as to the inspiring thoughts it contains, its lessons on morality and piety, or its incentives to duty and self-sacrifice. No where else will such heroic unselfishness be found, both taught in the loftiest forms and exemplified in the most perfect life. Men have drawn from this book for centuries inspiration for personal living and public teaching, and it is still the one deep inexhaustible well of salvation and instruction. The greatest of modern Englishmen modeled his style upon it; the most distinguished of modern orators drew from it his inspiration; the late laureate poet of Britain learned in its school the art of poesy; the foremost of theologians discovered in it the materials for their systems; and, above all, God-like character—the noblest cathedral structure ever reared among men—finds both its living stones in its quarry and its pattern in its mount of vision. By it human lives have been transfigured, and even worldly society unconsciously and unwillingly revolutionized. While other books inform, and some few reform, this one Book transforms.

(4.) The Bible is not only first but last of all books—Alpha and Omega—in the alphabet of the ages. It outlives all the ancient literature, alone indestructible and imperishable. God is its authority, and its lifetime is Eternity. Immortality is stamped upon it. Burned in a thousand fires of persecution, every effort has been made not only to destroy it as a book, but to exterminate it as a moral force among men, to blot out its record even from their memories. But it not only survives, but, like the Incarnate Word, has the keys of death and hades; it multiplies as its enemies seek to annihilate it. To-day, after eighteen centuries of antagonism, it is the widest spread and read of all books, the best known, translated into over four hundred tongues, and found wherever man opens the door to a new civilization.

The Bible is like the banyan tree; its very branches bend down and take root. It spreads over whole continents, and could not be eradicated without tearing up the very soil of society. When Sir David Dalyrimple, whose mind and culture fitted him for such a task, undertook to find how far the New Testament had embedded itself in the literature of the first three centuries, he found nearly

251

every verse. Where there is such pervasiveness,
there must be power. To-day it is estimated that
one-third of all our current literature treats of it
directly, as in commentaries and like books,
written to elucidate its contents; and another third
indirectly touches it by treating of Church history,
Christian biography, mission enterprise and kindred
topics. Of the remaining third, it may be safely
said that a large part of it in some form is moulded
or affected by the Bible, though only written to
assault it.

(5.) These are thus God's Living Oracles. The
Word of God is powerful because it is quick—alive
—living and life-giving. It "liveth and abideth
forever." It is a mirror, but such a mirror as the
retina of the eye with its network of living nerves.
It is a seed, but a seed that hides in its heart the
vital principle of God's life, yielding, wherever
sown, a harvest of souls into life eternal. It is a
sword, but with power to pierce to the dividing
asunder of soul and spirit, joints and marrow, and
discern the thoughts and intents of the heart. It
is a living counsellor,* wisely answering inquiries
and solving practical problems—the only true living oracle, that without resorting to a deceptive
ambiguity, solves our perplexities.

* Psalm cxix: 24.

The Ethics of God

A strange, mysterious life pervades this Book, which makes it not only an inexplicable mystery, but an indestructible book. It is also life giving. Its living waters make everything to live, wherever this river of God cometh. The living Spirit of God here speaks to the responsive spirit of man. And so down through the ages this Book continues to go, a mighty miracle worker, forever undying in itself, and carrying to the nations a message and a power which are both divine.

In bringing these chapters to a conclusion, there is one position that affects not only the whole argument, but is intimately linked with all rational conviction, both as to the inspired verities of the Word of God and the deity and atoning work of the Lord Jesus Christ. It must be remembered that to demand mathematical proof upon moral questions is absurd, since mathematical proof concerns the science of quantity, and moral proof admits of no demonstration stronger or more convincing than what is called moral probability. In other words, there are many things that cannot be demonstrated except on the grounds of high probability; yet we have no hesitation in accepting such conclusions, though they are not susceptible of mathematical demonstration.

This fact, however, should never affect the

security of our confidence in the certainties of our holy faith. It has long been a settled and admitted canon of philosophy, that, whenever a hypothesis is found which proves adequate to meet all the facts of the case, all the factors of the problem, it is safe to adopt it as the accurate solution of the difficulty. Further than this, if a hypothesis which does not meet and explain all the facts for which explanation is sought, yet serves to unravel the mystery better and more satisfactorily than any other, it is to be held fast as, at least, an approximate solution, until a better and more perfect solution is suggested.

This was the exact method whereby Johann Kepler, one of the greatest astronomers of all ages, in the 16th century solved some of the most difficult problems of astronomy. Up to his day, the character of the planetary orbits, with the kindred questions of their comparative areas and times of revolution, were unsettled and perplexing problems. For years he attentively studied these great questions, and made and applied eighteen successive hypotheses to their solution—as a locksmith would successively apply as many keys to the unlocking of some complicated door. At last, it occurred to him to suppose the planets to move in ellipses rather than in circular orbits, the sun being one of the foci of the ellipse. This hypothesis was found to be perfectly reconcilable with all observed facts and phenomena. His enthusiasm was unbounded, and he exclaimed, "I am thinking, O Almighty God, Thy thoughts after Thee!" He saw that God had waited for thousands of years for an accurate observer to explain these phenomena. He then began to experiment until he discovered a second law, namely, that the radius-vector sweeps over equal areas in equal times. Then he discovered his third law, but only after twenty-two years of vigorou application, namely—that the square of the periodic time is proportional to the cube of the mean distance. Thus, upon the principle of what is called adequate hypothesis, he made these great astronomical discoveries of the laws and principles of planetary and stellar motion, and determined the mean distances of the planets from the sun, and their respective rates of revolution. Upon such questions as these there can be no scientific certainty, but, at most, only a high degree of probability. But, ever since his day, these explanations, known as Kepler's three great laws, have been accepted as the truth, even by scientific men, without any hesitation or even doubt, because his hypothesis proved adequate to unlock the doors of the heavens.

God's Living Oracles

There is a great mystery investing the Old Testament prophecies, and the New Testament histories. The greatest of all moral and spiritual phenomena is the person of the Son of God, the Saviour of men. For these great mysteries, there is but one adequate hypothesis, but one key that unlocks the door to this Temple of Truth. That hypothesis supposes the Bible to be a divinely inspired book, in every part, bearing the impress of divine intelligence and wisdom; that holy men of old spake as they were moved by the Holy Ghost, as the mouthpiece of God, the only true Speaker— that Omniscience communicated to them an accurate forecast of future events, and that He who came as the fulfilment of all this great body of prophecy was none other than the Son of God as well as the Son of man—identical with man in His humanity, identical with the Father in His character and attributes, history and destiny.

When that hypothesis is accepted and adopted, the mystery of the Old and New Testaments is adequately unravelled and explained; above all, the mystery of the God-Man finds its only satisfactory solution. If that hypothesis be rejected, we are left in inextricable difficulty. When one has lived in the atmosphere of certain conviction, under the power of a deep persuasion that this book is the Word of God, that Jesus Christ is the Son of God and the Saviour of men, amid all the disturbing doubts and perplexities of this age of negation and opposition, he calmly sings, like a lark in the midst of the storm:

> "Let all the forms that men devise
>   Assault my faith with treacherous art,
> I'll call them vanity and lies,
>   And bind Thy Gospel to my heart."

Origin of matter - not eternal -
God - atheism refuted -

[illegible handwritten annotations in margins: "is reached out", "by chance", "Created", "God separate from creation", "Pantheism", "Matter", "refuted", "(41)"]

THE MODERN MISSION CENTURY
— VIEWED AS A CYCLE OF DIVINE WORKING

Rev. Arthur T. Pierson, D.D.,
Author of " Geo. Müller," " New Acts of the Apostles," etc.

Crown 8vo, cloth, $1.50 *net*

This is by all odds Dr. Pierson's strongest and most important work. It deals with the last century in the mission field. Its aim is not so much to give the annals of the century as to find the philosophy of its history—the centre about which all its events revolve. It studies the men and women, occurrences and developments, as divinely appointed and adjusted to mission work.

" Dr. Pierson has written this book with fulness of detail, yet with such a judicious grouping of his materials and with so much fervor and enthusiasm as to make the reading of his narrative at once easy and inspiring. It is a noble and convincing record of Christian faith and achievement."—*Living Age.*

" A large personal element in copious illustrations drawn from the experiences of a multitude of men and women in the mission field imparts peculiar interest to this volume."—*Outlook.*

The Baker & Taylor Co., Publishers
33-37 E. 17th Street, Union Square North, New York